To all those, known and unknown,
Quaker and non-Quaker,
Irish, English, American and others,
who gave so much of their energies,
and sometimes their health or their lives,
in an attempt to assist those who
suffered in the Great Famine in Ireland

**"...believing that many individuals in districts not so heavily afflicted and in England may be found who would be glad to impart of their abundance if a suitable channel were presented to them, the formation of a central committee to receive subscriptions, distribute funds where particularly needed, and communicate information ... has closely engaged our attention."**

*Letter from Joseph Bewley to Quakers in Ireland, 2nd November 1846*

**"William Forster ... offered ... to go over to Ireland ... to discover trustworthy and suitable channels ..."**

*Address of the Committee of Members of the Society of Friends in England, 2nd December 1846*

# PREFACE

Quaker work during Ireland's great famine is one of the most familiar aspects of Quakerism in the public mind and throughout the country there are strong folk memories of Quaker relief during that major crisis. While a certain amount has been written about these efforts to date there has been no book that is reasonably comprehensive and, at the same time, comparatively short and accessible to the general reader. As a result the story of the involvement of the Society of Friends has not been fully understood.

Throughout this volume there are references to the Society of Friends, which was the official title of the organisation in the last century. Today, the full title is the Religious Society of Friends, though the term *Quaker* is in general use, particularly by those who are not Quakers. The terms *Friend* and *Quaker* are both commonly used to mean "member of the Society of Friends".

The Religious Society of Friends is still active and thriving in Ireland, Britain and throughout the world today and many of the attributes of the 19th century Quakers may still be traced in modern members of the Society. Quakers have always been involved in charitable works, initially amongst their own members, and later amongst disadvantaged sections of society. Long before the famine relief works Quakers were campaigning for the abolition of slavery, prison reform and better conditions for workers in factories and relief work was undertaken among victims of a crisis in the 1770's with civilians caught up in the American war of independence. Since the famine Friends have been involved in many similar activities such as helping victims of wars, feeding the hungry and overseas aid.

Today in Britain and Ireland Quaker work continues, both through the involvement of individual Quakers in a variety of charitable organisations and through the work of various committees of the Society itself. "Irish Quaker Faith in Action" is involved in assisting projects overseas in places such as the Gaza Strip, Zambia, Kenya, Vietnam and Buskina Fasa in Upper Volta. The help given includes money, equipment and Irish Quaker personnel. Working within Ireland itself, Friends have established projects in the north to help to break down barriers between communities and this includes the provision of facilities for visitors to the Maze and Maghaberry Prisons such as canteens and children's playrooms. There is also Quaker Cottage in Belfast where people from both sides of the community meet and get to know each other through activities such as mother and children's

# A SUITABLE CHANNEL

## Quaker Relief in the Great Famine

**Rob Goodbody**

**P**ale———
**Publishing**

1995

First published in Ireland in 1995 by
Pale Publishing, Old Bawn, Old Connaught, Bray

ISBN 0 9522663 2 6

Printed in Ireland by Central Remedial Clinic Training Unit

groups, children's holidays, lunch clubs and so forth. Irish Friends are also involved with Quaker Peace and Service, a London-based organisation which represents Quakers in Britain and Ireland and which maintains a wide variety of projects throughout the world.

The Religious Society of Friends is one of the smaller parts of the Christian church and has a very simple approach to Christianity with a minimum of rules, regulations and ceremony. A fundamental feature of Quakerism is the recognition that God is present in each person - probably one of the main reasons why Quakers have always been so ready to help others who are in distress.

## Units of measurement

I must apologise for the seemingly haphazard use of different units of measurement in this book. At the time of the famine the old Irish measures were still in general use, though statute measure had become official. Land areas tended to be given in Irish acres, which were considerably larger than statute acres, as were roods and perches, while the statute mile had more or less replaced the Irish mile. We are in an equivalent state today, with imperial measure still commonly used, though metric units have been the official measure since 1983. As a result, any figure that I have calculated myself is given in modern units, while any I have quoted from elsewhere are given in whatever units appeared in the original. The Irish acre was about 1.6 statute acres and this was roughly two thirds of a hectare. Weight in pounds was equivalent to about 0.45 kilograms, while the difference between tons and tonnes is so small as to be irrelevant in this book.

# CONTENTS

# ACKNOWLEDGEMENTS

I was asked to write a booklet on the Ireland's Great Hunger as one of a series explaining the various embroidered panels in the Quaker Tapestry which illustrate many different aspects of Quakerism. These panels are on display in the Quaker Tapestry and Exhibition Centre at Kendal in Cumbria and are the fruits of eight years labour by about 4,000 Quakers in ten countries. During the course of the research and writing of the booklet I became aware that there was also need for a somewhat longer book which would still be accessible to the general reader and I am grateful to those involved with the Quaker Tapestry, particularly Melanie Barber and Edward H. Milligan, for expressing enthusiasm rather than horror at the thought of me producing a second work on the same theme.

The request for the Quaker Tapestry booklet came through the Historical Committee of the Religious Society of Friends in Ireland and my thanks are due to the committee for nominating me to undertake the work and for being supportive of my idea for this companion volume. A great deal of work was carried out in the Friends Historical Library at Swanbrook in Donnybrook, Dublin where I received great help from the curator, Mary Shackleton, and the staff of the library, Verity E. Murdoch, the late Stella M. B. Webb, Belinda Jacob and Elizabeth M. Pearson and the last mentioned, in particular, used her extensive knowledge of the library sources to find numerous snippets of useful information for me.

A number of members of the Friends Historical Committee and others provided useful comments and encouragement, including Maurice J. Wigham, Desmond G. Neill, Christopher Moriarty, Philip R. Jacob, Richard S. Harrison, J. Glynn Douglas, Helen M. Haughton and my father, John G. Goodbody. Joan C. Johnson provided a wealth of comments based on her research into Quaker relief work in Waterford.

Kevin Devally of Colmanstown, Co. Galway, was most helpful in showing me over the buildings which remain from the Quaker model farm and my thanks are also due to Martin T. Kelly who invited me there.

The usual thanks also go to the National Archives in Bishop Street where so many of the records of the Quaker relief committees may be found.

For the illustrations I am grateful to Jonathan P. Wigham for the photographs of Richard D. Webb and Jonathan Pim, to the Friends Historical Library for the photograph of the meeting house in Eustace Street and for the reproductions of documents, and Elaine Tagliarino for the illustrations of the relief ships which appeared in the *Pictorial Times* in January and April 1847.

**Rob Goodbody**
**Old Bawn, Old Connaught, Bray**                                          **29 June 1995**

# CHAPTER ONE:

# DISASTER APPROACHES

The Great Famine in Ireland in the 1840's was one of the worst natural disasters to have occurred in modern Europe. Within a comparatively short period, Ireland lost about one quarter of its population through famine, disease and emigration. Just as importantly, Irish society was radically changed by the devastation of the population at the poorer end of the social scale and the increase in political motivation amongst those who remained.

The population of Europe had been increasing rapidly in the decades prior to the 1840's but for reasons that are not entirely understood Ireland's population grew at a rate that was much faster than average. By 1841, Ireland had a population of 8.17 million and while there is some question as to the size of the population at the start of the famine, it was certainly significantly greater than this.

While Ireland had some industry in the mid 19th century, chiefly, but not exclusively, in the north east, it was, on the whole, an agricultural country. The system of land tenure was quite different to that which applied in the rest of the United Kingdom and a very significant proportion of people lived on a subsistence basis with no security of tenure over their small plots of land. Over the previous century or so the Irish labourers and small farmers had come to rely more and more on the potato for their food as this crop could feed more people per acre than other crops and did not require any significant investment in the improvement of the land. This reliance on the potato was not exclusive to Ireland, Scottish labourers also used potatoes a great deal and even in England there was an increasing tendency for labourers to live on potatoes. In Ireland, however, the dependence was far greater than elsewhere and a higher proportion of people had little else in their diet.

It was inevitable that this reliance on a single crop would lead to problems any time that the potato did not produce its expected yield and any large scale shortfall would be catastrophic. There had been famines in Ireland on many occasions before, particularly from 1739 to 1741 and in 1800-01, 1816-17, 1822 and 1831. In many other years there had been partial or localised failures of the potato. On these occasions systems of government and voluntary relief had been set up that had kept the problem under reasonable control. It was only a matter of time, though, until a worse failure happened and in the autumn of 1845 it finally did.

## 1845: Partial failure

In the autumn of 1845 a new disease appeared among the Irish potato crops that was to become known as potato blight. In a very short time it caused widespread damage, visibly destroying the green portions of the potato plants and leaving an unmistakable stench, while the tuber itself was turned into a foul-smelling mush. Although the disease had been reported elsewhere before this, it seems to have taken Ireland by surprise. The reaction was disbelief at first, but fairly soon the extent of the problem was appreciated and measures were adopted for assisting those who were left without food.

While the effects of the disease were dramatic the crop was only partially affected. Using the experience of previous potato shortages the government set up a system of relief to provide food and employment. A Relief Commission was set up to administer grants to local relief committees which would look after aid in local areas. Substantial amounts of maize were purchased from America to supply to these committees and public works were established to provide employment to the destitute on projects such as roads and harbour improvements.

Voluntary bodies were also involved in famine relief at this stage, notably a body set up in Dublin known as the Mansion House Committee. Other agencies were set up in cities in the United States to send help.

By the time that the new harvest was due in the summer of 1846 it could be seen that while the relief measures had been far from free of problems, they had been largely successful. It is now thought that very few people died in the 1845-46 season as a result of the destruction caused by the potato blight. This failure had been only partial though, and it would have been clear that the relief system could not have succeeded if the destruction of the crop had been more widespread. In the autumn of 1846 this was to be the case and the famine entered a more severe phase.

## 1846: Total failure

In August 1846 the news broke that the potato crop had again succumbed to the blight and that this time the destruction was virtually complete. In September *The Times* reported that:

> what was last year but a partial destruction is now a total annihilation; and it is become very general belief that the month of December will not find a single potato in the country. Ireland is, therefore, doomed to suffer a recurrence (if it should not rather be called a continuance) of that distress which has well nigh pauperised the whole population.

The entire system for famine relief was changed at this stage. This was due in part to the change of government with the consequent shift in policy and it was partly due to the scale of the problem which needed to be tackled. It was quite clear that the problem was far larger than could be managed by any government, given the political beliefs of the day, but the attitudes adopted by the Whig government showed little understanding of the Irish situation. In the later stage of the crisis the cost of their relief works were to be levied on the local areas even though those areas most in need were also the areas with the least resources. In the worst hit areas there was no network of merchants and shops through which food could be distributed and money was little used by those that lived a purely subsistence existence. On top of all of this, the winter of 1846-47 brought not only potato disease, but shortages of most of the grain crops throughout Europe so that government attempts to purchase food from abroad were up against intense competition from other European countries and prices were high. This also increased the political problem as it was feared that measures to relieve the Irish population would worsen the plight of English labourers.

In the light of the severity of the problem there was an increased amount of activity by individuals and voluntary bodies spurred by the constant reports in the newspapers and in magazines such as the *Illustrated London News* and the *Gardener's Chronicle*. Various organisations came into existence in the autumn of 1846 as the situation worsened and the food shortages were resulting in public unrest in many parts of Ireland. Inevitably, members of the Society of Friends were among those who reacted at this time.

# CHAPTER TWO:

# ESTABLISHING RELIEF COMMITTEES

In the mid 19th century the Society of Friends as a body did not tend to involve itself directly in social issues such as charitable works. Individual members of the Society certainly did, and by this time Friends had become well known for their activities. Due to the way in which the Society is run by its members rather than by a hierarchy or priesthood it is often difficult, particularly for the non-Friend, to distinguish the activities of the Society from those of its individual members. From the point of view of the historian this creates a problem in that records are incomplete. The Religious Society of Friends is well known for its comprehensive and complete records such as minute books and birth, marriage and death records. However, when Friends were acting in their individual capacity they would not always have left such records and their work may now be forgotten. The Central Relief Committee of the Society of Friends in Ireland left a relatively comprehensive account of its works and while this give a clear picture of these activities the balance is distorted by the lack of any similar records for the local activities of individuals and small committees.

## The Central Relief Committee

At the beginning of November 1846 a Dublin Quaker, Joseph Bewley, wrote to Quakers throughout Ireland pointing out that the serious situation facing the country needed careful consideration and that Friends might wish to consider the establishment of a committee to organise some form of relief. On 13th November 1846 a meeting of members of the Society of Friends was convened in the Quaker Meeting house in Eustace Street in Dublin to consider what they could do to assist the situation. At that meeting it was decided that rather than join in the efforts of other groups they would form their own body which was to be known as the Central Relief Committee of the Society of Friends. This committee was to have two main objects, namely the raising of funds for distribution and the gathering of information regarding the nature of the problem in different areas so that the best means of relief could be devised.

The meeting appointed twenty-one Friends to the Central Relief Committee, giving them power of co-option. Care was taken in selecting members to include some who had commercial contacts throughout Ireland in order to help in the gathering of information. This committee was instructed to establish a network of correspondents drawn from members of the Society elsewhere in Ireland in order to help in keeping in touch with the country at large. Twenty-one corresponding members were appointed from places as far apart as Belfast and Cork but with no members in the west of the country, reflecting the lack of Quakers living there.

*The large Meeting Room at the former Quaker Meeting House, Eustace Street, Dublin.*

While the Central Relief Committee was established by a meeting of individual Friends rather than by the Society of Friends itself, this was not the case in Munster. The Society of Friends in Ireland is organised on a system which groups individual meeting houses for the purposes of decision making. A fairly local group meets once a month and is known as a *Monthly Meeting*. This reports to a *Quarterly Meeting* which is based on one of the three provinces of Ulster, Munster and Leinster, the fourth province, Connaught, not having a significant population of Friends. The highest level of decision making for the whole of Ireland, roughly equivalent to a synod in other churches, is the *Yearly Meeting*. In November 1846 Cork Monthly Meeting decided to establish a relief committee and in December 1846, as we shall see later, this committee was distributing relief in the south west. In the following month, at the behest of the Central Relief Committee, Munster Quarterly Meeting decided that it would establish three further committees to act, with the Cork committee, as auxiliary committees of the Central Relief Committee to organise famine relief. These committees were based on the Monthly Meetings which constituted Munster Quarterly Meeting, namely Cork, Limerick, Waterford and Clonmel and they acted as the gatherers of information and administrators of relief within the province of Munster, thereby taking an enormous burden off the central committee. The four auxiliary committees in Munster had between eight and twelve members each and were given very specific areas to administer. This took in the whole of the province of Munster and spread well beyond it to take in the counties of Wexford and Kilkenny as well as a small but significant portion of county Galway.

### The Committee of Friends in London

At the same time that Dublin Friends decided to call a meeting to discuss famine relief Friends in England were thinking along similar lines, but independently. Unlike the Dublin committee, the impetus for the London response came from the Society itself, through its business committee known as the Meeting for Sufferings. On 6th November 1846 that meeting decided to convene a meeting of men Friends in and about London to consider the matter, collect information and raise subscriptions. This meeting took place on 9th November and decided that the best course of action was to write to Friends in Ireland to announce that they had decided to raise funds and to ask what would be the best way in which they could provide assistance. The Central Relief Committee replied, painting a bleak picture of the prospect facing Ireland, explaining the huge task facing Friends, particularly in relation to the more remote districts, and it asked for advice and assistance.

As a result of this exchange of letters a second meeting was held in London on 25th November and amongst those attending were Friends from Ireland who told the meeting of the sufferings of the Irish people. At this meeting the *Committee of the Society of Friends in London* was established. This body consisted of twenty Quakers who were charged with the responsibility for issuing an address to Friends in Great Britain and raising a "liberal subscription" throughout the nation.

Throughout the period of Friends' relief work in the great hunger the two committees worked closely together, members of each frequently travelling to attend meetings of the other, and helping to gather information and spread publicity.

# CHAPTER THREE:

# SEEKING QUAKER SUPPORT

### Address of the Central Relief Committee

The first action taken by the two committees was to produce "addresses" to the members of the Society in the two islands. The Dublin committee published its address on 30th November, printing 4,500 copies, of which 300 were sent to the London committee. This address acknowledged the efforts of government bodies to tackle the problem but regretted that this was not being matched by the efforts of the inhabitants of the various districts. An example of energetic, united and well directed effort by independent individuals of all classes was considered to be highly important as the scale of the disaster was beyond the capabilities of any government to tackle on its own. The committee acknowledged that Friends were setting up local groups to provide relief and urged them to continue. However, it was also pointed out that a central system was very important, particularly in view of the considerable part of Ireland where there were no Quakers living and which were badly in need of assistance. Friends were encouraged to donate to the central fund, but it was made clear that this should not be at the expense of local efforts, only those who had funds to spare after looking after their own districts should contribute.

The address also outlined the forms of relief which were being considered and emphasised that care would have to be taken in all relief work to avoid interference with the normal traffic of provisions. This is an attitude which was also held by the government and has been heavily criticised. However, the reality of famine conditions is that the entire economy of the country is severely damaged so that it is not only those who depend on the potato that suffer and die, but gradually the effects are felt through the whole population. If relief works are introduced indiscriminately they could destroy the network of merchants and retailers on which the country normally depends so that a longer term problem is created.

The first option for famine relief outlined in the address was to encourage the establishment of soup kitchens in towns and thickly inhabited places in order to provide a cheap and nutritious kind of diet. Secondly, grants would be made available to local relief committees and trustworthy individuals, subject to the necessary vetting.

The final comment in the Dublin committee's address was a salutary one. At that time no one understood how the potato had been destroyed and it was to be many years before blight was recognised to be a fungal infection. The committee pointed out that this event could not have been predicted, nor could anyone presume that similar visitations would not appear in other crops:

> It needs but the turning of the same Almighty Hand, to spread sickness and desolation where health and abundance now dwell. Let none presume to think, that the summons to deep and serious thoughtfulness, and to a close searching of heart, does not extend to him. We may justly regard this event as a call to humiliation; and in contrasting the habits of luxury of the rich with the poverty always existing around them, who can venture to say that 'pride and fullness of bread' are not, in the case of this nation, as in that of a people formerly, amongst our prominent offences in the Divine sight?

## Address of the London Committee

On 2nd December 1846 the London committee published its address, 500 copies of which were sent to the Dublin committee. This suggested that Friends in each district should assemble to hear the address and that a committee be appointed to collect subscriptions. Even before this date Friends in Great Britain had offered contributions of more than £5,600 and these were listed at the close of the document.

This address set down the basic facts to the Friends of Great Britain explaining that a famine existed in Ireland, though using the word with caution. While admitting that there was plenty of food in Ireland, the address explained that this food was not accessible to a large proportion of the population and that the wages people were earning on the public works were not enough to offset the rises in food prices. Care was taken to explain that the difference between support for the poor in Ireland and England when describing the misery:

> For those whose dependence was on this crop, and who have no money to buy other food, the failure of the potato is necessarily

the failure of all; and must, if timely aid be not supplied, produce starvation. What is this but famine to this class of people, who form, be it remembered, in some parts the entire population of the district; and not, like the poor in England, with neighbours in wealthy or in easy circumstances interspersed among them, and ready to hold out the hand of help.

Lest anyone think that the activities of the government to tackle the hunger removed the need for private charity, the address explained how the system could only provide relief for a certain section of society while others had no means of support from government or other agencies. Looking further into the future, it was hoped that plans may be set on foot that would lead to a longer term improvement in the lot of the Irish peasantry.

On a more sombre note the address, like its Dublin counterpart, recognised that Friends could not relieve the famine but merely assist a proportion of the starving:

If there be one thousand of our fellow men who would perish if nothing were done, our rescue of one hundred from destruction is surely not the less a duty and a privilege, because there are other nine hundred whom we cannot save.

In an appeal that echoes those of today's relief agencies, the address put the amounts of subscribers' money into perspective thus: "Every £100 subscribed ... may supply food for two months for fifty families, or three hundred individuals, who might otherwise die of hunger." The appeal finished with "And may we all remember the words of the Lord Jesus, how he said 'It is more blessed to give than to receive'".

Appended to the London committee's address were several extracts from letters received from correspondents all around Ireland describing the state of the people in the country and how assistance could be offered to relieve the distress.

## Address to American Friends

Once the Dublin committee's address was completed a copy was sent to Quakers in Philadelphia with a view to mustering support in that quarter.

This was followed by a letter from the London committee to Friends in North America to inform them of the situation. This described the state of the country and the prospects for the huge numbers of people whose food supply had been ruined. It went on to relate how the two committees had been set up and how the Dublin committee was by now operating an efficient system for relief. The address ended with a brief and direct plea:

> We hear that you have, during the past year, been blessed with fruitful harvests in many parts of your continent; and we wish, in thus communicating with you, not only to enlist your sympathies, but to open the way for your co-operation; and to invite you, in the exercise of that enlarged commiseration which you will doubtless feel, to aid us in this work, by the supply of either food or money, as you may think fit.

# CHAPTER FOUR:

# ORGANISATION AND PREMISES

Within the first month of its existence the Central Relief Committee had appointed its own secretaries and treasurers, set up its organisation of corresponding members, produced its address to the Quakers of Ireland and begun to receive subscriptions. Many of the members of the committee were merchants who were experienced in the distribution of goods and in the proper management of goods and accounts. All were members of the Society of Friends which is a religious body which has no clergy and no hierarchy but has always been operated on the basis that all members have an involvement in the running of the organisation. In practice this has been done through an elaborate network of committees at local, regional and national level so that the establishment of an efficient and flexible structure of committees and subcommittees would have been second nature to those on the Central Relief Committee. It is also an important factor that the Society of Friends is a relatively small body so that its members would know other Quakers throughout the country from having served on committees with them and attended meetings in other areas. Quakers tended to marry within the Society so that they would also have had family relationships with Quakers all over the country. As a result there was a ready-made network of personal contacts wherever in Ireland there were Quakers and this would have made the task of gleaning information or checking local facts all the easier.

Throughout the period of its existence the Central Relief Committee formed a large number of subcommittees to carry out specific tasks. Some would have been short lived and been little more than the appointment of three or four committee members for a single short term task such as finding premises. Others had more complex and long term tasks and have left significant records of their operations.

We must not forget that the Quaker relief committees were made up of ordinary people who had little or no experience of such work. They were highly motivated by feelings for fellow human beings and by a spirit of God within, but there was no predetermined system on which to operate. The impetus for the establishment of the organisation was that Friends saw a gap between, on the one hand, the large numbers of people who wanted to help financially or otherwise and, on the other, the enormity of the destitution in the afflicted areas. The idea was that the Quaker committees would bridge that gap by providing what Joseph Bewley referred to as "a suitable channel" for the receiving of subscriptions and distribution of funds in accordance with information collected. Resolving to do this was one thing, implementing it was another.

For the first few weeks of its existence the committee was uncertain how to go about its task. A subcommittee was set up at the end of November 1846 to decide on the best way of providing relief to areas which were at a distance from the homes of any members of the Society and it took about three weeks to formulate its report. In the meantime the decision was taken to establish a soup shop in Dublin and an English Quaker, William Forster, arrived in Dublin en route to the west where he would be granting aid.

In the middle of December the Central Relief Committee felt it was able to set down the basis on which it would work. It was recognised that the amount of business it would handle would be large and would need an efficient system of operation. For this purpose it was decided to rent an office, staffed by a clerk to be engaged by the week or month so as to act as assistant secretary and accountant. The period of rental was to be for 10 to 12 months and it should be borne in mind that there was no reason to believe at this time that the famine would last more than the current farming year until the next harvest. The fundamental work of the committee was to be carried out by a subcommittee of seven Friends which was to sit not less than three days a week and if the business was heavy it should sit daily, Sunday excepted. This subcommittee was to keep regular minutes and to receive applications for assistance and report on each application to the next general committee meeting and to facilitate the assessment of applications an application form was to be drafted and printed. The members of this subcommittee were to be the treasurers of the Central Relief Committee, James Perry and Thomas Pim junior, the two secretaries, Jonathan Pim and Joseph Bewley (who was also a treasurer), and three ordinary members, Edward Barrington, Adam Woods and Thomas H. Todhunter. There was to be a quorum of three, which contrasts with the Central Relief Committee which had no quorum and sometimes met with only one member present!

The standing subcommittee found a suitable office at 57 William Street, Dublin, consisting of a small office fronting the street on the ground floor and a larger one over it. The ground floor room would be suitable as a public office to be occupied by the assistant secretary while the upper floor was to be the committee room. Both rooms were available to let fully furnished at a rent of £7 per quarter. William Hughes was appointed to the job of assistant secretary and accountant on a part time basis while he also held a job in a public company, the duties of which were not considered to be likely to materially interfere with his work for the committee. He was to be paid £2 a week. From February he was joined by Richard Barrington, a Dublin Friend who volunteered to work in the office and a few days later Richard Barrington was co-opted onto the Central Relief

57 William Street South, headquarters of the Central Relief Committee from December 1846 to April, 1847.

Committee to replace Samuel Watson who was stepping down.

At this stage the income to the committee from subscriptions was large and far outstripped the amount of relief being offered. The committee was aware of the fact that this level of subscriptions could not be sustained and that most of the funds would need to be held back and given out gradually as relief. The nature of the famine would lead to starvation and disease increasing over time to reach a peak in the summer of 1847 just before the harvest, following which, it was hoped, the problem would be over. For this reason the decision was taken to invest a substantial amount of the funds in some public security with a high rate of interest and £5,000 was invested in $3^1/_2\%$ Government Stock on 10 days recall. The committee later lent a substantial sum to the Mining Company of Ireland at a commercial rate of interest.

The possibilities of coming to arrangements with other relief organisations was also considered and an approach was received from another agency suggesting that relief work might be divided between the various agencies on a geographical basis. This suggestion was not pursued.

By March 1847 the immense workload was stretching the capabilities of the committee to its limits. Jonathan Pim, in particular, was suffering ill health from his onerous duties as Secretary and began to question the structure of their organisation, as a result of which the standing committee was restructured. Under the new arrangement it was to consist of twelve members, subdivided into three groups of four, each of which would take responsibility for the provision of relief in one of the provinces of Leinster, Ulster and Connaught - the fourth province of Munster already being catered for by auxiliary committees as we shall see. This subcommittee was to meet twice a week. Each of the three provinces was to have a secretary appointed from amongst its four committee members and the secretary was to have the power to make conditional grants of relief. To this end he was to attend the office every morning to inspect the correspondence, mark each letter as appropriate and make decisions on matters which did not need the ratification of the committee. These transactions were to be written up as far as possible each day to minimise the possibility of error. This was to be an onerous task for any voluntary helper, most of the committee members having their own jobs to attend to over and above the relief work. To assist this task further paid clerks were to be taken on, but they were to be kept to as small a number as was absolutely necessary. Consideration was also given to the possibility of engaging a paid secretary.

By April, as a result of the expansion in the work of the committee and, in particular, the enlargement of the staff and operations following the restructuring of the standing subcommittee, the premises in William Street were no longer adequate. New offices were leased at 43, Fleet Street,

Dublin from the committee responsible for the winding up of the recently-defunct Agricultural and Commercial Bank. The accommodation included the attic storey and the garret storey of the building with the use of the board room of the bank and an adjoining room for the purposes of committee meetings whenever those rooms were not required by the bank. The rent was to be £2 per week and one week's notice was required if the committee wished to vacate the premises or one month if the bank wanted to regain possession. The committee was also at liberty to employ the bank's porter or caretaker to clean out their rooms and offices, for which they would allow him 5 shillings a week.

# CHAPTER FIVE:

# FACT FINDING

## William Forster's journey in the west

One of the main tasks of the committees was to gather information about the state of the country. However, the network of corresponding Friends did not extend to the western parts of the country where the famine affected the most people and the solution to this problem was for individual Friends to undertake fact-finding tours in the more remote parts of the island. The first of these was William Forster, who had volunteered his services to the London committee at its meeting of 25th November 1846 and he set out almost immediately for Dublin. William Forster had been working among the poor of Norwich for a number of years and had gained considerable experience, most particularly in the operation of soup kitchens. He felt it to be his duty to travel to Ireland to assess the nature and extent of the disaster, to investigate channels for the distribution of relief and to assist in the setting up of soup kitchens.

Over the following four and a half months, William Forster travelled through some of the worst hit areas, accompanied at various times by English and Irish Friends. His tour brought him to the west and north west, through the counties of Roscommon, Leitrim, Fermanagh, Donegal, Sligo, Mayo, Galway, Longford and Cavan. Along the route he observed the extent of the destitution which he found to be much worse than he had expected. He took the trouble to encourage members of the local gentry to undertake relief works and he established links between the Central Relief Committee and local bodies and individuals that would help in the distribution of aid. William Forster had been given money before he set out so that he could intervene with immediate assistance wherever he thought it necessary.

The descriptions of what William Forster's party saw along their route were reported by members of his party such as Joseph Crosfield, James H. Tuke and William Edward Forster, son of William Forster, who had joined his father in Westport, Co Mayo in mid-January 1847. These reports told of large numbers of people working on government relief works to earn 8 pence per day, while food for a family would cost more than this at the inflated prices that famine had caused. They told of heart-rending scenes as people sought in vain to gain admission to the workhouses that were already full and they described children that were lethargic from hunger so that they could not even show interest in the arrival of strangers. Their accounts also took note of the state which the country had been in even before the famine struck, describing how existence was a struggle even in better times.

These accounts were invaluable in the way that they informed Friends in Dublin and, more particularly in England, of the perilous state of the country, dispelling any thoughts that previous accounts were distorted. William Edward Forster wrote:

> Bad as were my expectations, the reality far exceeded them. There is a prevailing idea in England, that the newspaper accounts are exaggerated. Particular cases may or may not be coloured, but no colouring can deepen the blackness of the truth.

## Edmund Richards's tour

Another visitor, in March 1847, was Edmund Richards, a Friend from Gloucester, who had arrived with a ship of provisions from Liverpool. Having discharged his cargo he and a member of the Limerick auxiliary committee toured in the counties of Clare, Limerick, Kerry and Cork.

## Tours by members of the Central Relief Committee

It was not only English Friends who toured in the more remote regions. In March 1847 two members of the Central Relief Committee, James Perry and Jonathan Pim visited Connaught. They described a number of soup kitchens in the Galway area, one of which was run by the local Protestant clergyman and others by the Sisters of Mercy and other convents. In other parts of the county of Galway they found relief measures in operation but there was also a great deal of distress. They reported that there were unwelcome effects of the government relief works in that the normal work carried out by the small farmers was being neglected as people were employed on the public works and were not cutting turf, fishing or collecting seaweed for manure.

In May 1847 Richard D. Webb, another member of the Central Relief Committee, toured Erris, one of the westernmost and most remote parts of Ireland. His purpose was to investigate allegations that some of the Committee's grants had been misappropriated and to distribute some of the committee's provisions which were stored at Belmullet, the principal town in Erris. He then went a little southwards to the island of Achill and then south again into the northern part of county Galway. He told of the starvation and the misery, of the breakdown of values in the face of famine, but remarked that while crime had increased in the form of the theft of food and livestock, he had come across no evidence of crime involving highway robbery or personal violence on land. He did, however, describe acts of piracy upon the seas when the small fishing boats had surrounded passing ships which carried provisions and had robbed them of any food on board.

*Richard D. Webb*

## Inspections by the Auxiliary Committees

It was not only the London and Dublin Committees that had reports from members travelling in the remote parts of Ireland. The auxiliary committees in Munster also sent deputations into the rural areas to assess the state of the districts in which they intended to make aid available. The visiting Friends included Thomas Wright, Joseph Harvey and William Harvey for the Cork committee, Robert Davis for the Clonmel committee and James Harvey and Thomas Grubb for the Limerick committee. These travellers reported that fishermen were finding it difficult to continue their work through lack of food for their families when they were out fishing and through having insufficient clothing for the conditions at sea. They also told of how they had not seen any preparations being made for the following year's crops with the obvious fear that whether or not the potato disease returned there would not be enough food for the coming season. Scenes of human misery formed an inevitable part of their findings, just as was encountered by those who travelled in any other part of the west.

## James Hack Tuke in Connaught

James H. Tuke, a Quaker from York, had been one of William Forster's companions in the first tour of the west of Ireland after the establishment of the relief committees. In the autumn of 1847 he returned to carry out another tour. He visited Mayo and wrote an account for English Friends describing the nature of this large, but under-developed county. Here he found that the workhouse at Ballina was up to fifty miles from some parts of the district which it served and he compared the scale of facilities in Mayo with parts of England in an effective illustration of the inadequate provision of services for the relief of the poor.

Just as he had done on his previous visit, James Hack Tuke wrote vivid accounts of the districts he visited with clear explanations of the workings of the land system and how it contributed to the causes of the famine.

# CHAPTER SIX:

# FUNDS AND DONATIONS

As the purpose of the Quaker relief committees was to channel aid from those who were offering it towards those who needed it the raising of funds would be a crucial part of the effort. Assistance was offered in the first instance from Quakers themselves and at the meeting in Dublin which set up the Central Relief Committee no less than £1,705 was donated by members of the Society of Friends - equivalent to more than £90,000 at today's prices. The London committee was also taking in substantial funds and by the end of 1846 it had received more than £20,000. While the bulk of this money had come from members of the Society of Friends there was also a significant proportion from non-members and the committee decided that it would willingly become trustee for any such funds.

Subscriptions continued to come in over the early months of 1847 and by the time of the Yearly Meeting of the Society of Friends in Ireland in May 1847 a total of £4,800 had been collected from Irish Quakers, £35,500 from English Quakers and £4,000 from non-Quakers in both countries.

Donations received from the United States exceeded those from the United Kingdom and ultimately formed the bulk of the resources available to the committees. In response to the copies of the Dublin committee's address which had been sent to a Friend in New York, subscriptions were sought by American Quakers and the first result was the sum of £500 which was sent from Philadelphia Friends at the end of December 1846. The address sent from the London committee at the beginning of the following month to Friends in North America helped to spread the news of the extent of the suffering and the need for subscriptions and before long donations were being offered from people of all religions and all backgrounds throughout the United States.

A major influence on the aid which was sent from the United States was a letter from Jonathan Pim to Jacob Harvey, a New York Quaker. This letter was written at the beginning of January 1847 and recounted some of the scenes which Jonathan Pim had seen when he was in Mayo with William Forster. He explained that:

in the parts of Mayo which I visited, the failure [of the potato] is complete, and the destruction of the cottier population is total. They have nothing. The public works do not employ one quarter of them. There is no other employment. The wages of those who do get work ... are quite insufficient to support a family at present prices. They have been unable to purchase their usual supply of winter clothing, and numbers have been forced by want to pawn any good clothes they had. The pigs are gone; the poultry are eaten or sold; the very dogs have been drowned, lest they should eat anything that would support human life.

Jacob Harvey published this letter and it aroused considerable sympathy throughout the United States. It was also important in persuading the relief committees in America to entrust their donations to the Dublin committee for distribution.

By May 1847 the financial contributions sent from North America had amounted to £15,000. A far greater operation was the donation of food, though this did not arrive so soon as the money, due to three months of adverse weather which prevented sailing ships from leaving for Europe. The first consignment of food arrived in Cork on 10th April 1847 carrying Indian meal from New York and within less than a month about twenty ships had left the United States carrying the equivalent of about 30,000 barrels of meal. Over the next year some 91 ships arrived from the United States carrying 9,911 tons of food with a value of £133,847. Almost half of this came from New York (4,658 tons), followed by Philadelphia with 2,052 tons, New Orleans with 1,740 tons and the rest in smaller quantities from several other ports. By far the largest contribution came from the Irish Relief Committee in New York and this committee also forwarded supplies on behalf of smaller organisations in inland towns and cities.

The decision to send food rather than money was a deliberate one as the harvest of 1846 had been bad in general throughout Europe so that there was a general shortage of grains and other foods. Most European countries were trying to purchase food on the international market and this pushed the prices up. A large amount of the donations from the American people was in food and to this was added food purchased by American Quakers using the substantial cash donations. Initially there was a problem of a lack of available shipping to carry the supplies to Ireland but once this was overcome the bulk of the remittances from North America came in food rather than money.

*An American war ship, the Jamestown delivering relief supplies at Cork, April, 1847.*

One problem with providing food donations was that the cost of shipment was vastly greater than for cash donations. This was solved when the various freight and railway companies throughout the United States allowed supplies for Ireland to be carried without charge. The remaining major cost would then be the shipment of the supplies across the Atlantic and with this in mind the London committee approached the government to ask for assistance. The government agreed to pay the cost of all shipments of American donations to the Quaker committees and in all this amounted to more than £33,000.

Donations of clothing were also sent from America, and ultimately a total of 642 packages was received in addition to 210 bales of clothing received from England.

The raising of funds to meet the needs of the committee's relief work was not without its problems, including the issue of ethics. The Central Relief Committee was established and run by members of the Society of Friends and, as would be expected, was run on the basis of that Society's principles. Slavery was an issue on which Friends had campaigned over many years and this was a strongly held conviction in the 1840's when slaves were so much a part of the economy of the southern United States and the Caribbean islands. When the cities of Baltimore and Charleston sent £1,200 and £1,300 respectively for the funds a great controversy began. Several members of the Central Relief Committee wanted the donations to be returned on principle but their views were outweighed by those who wished to accept the gifts. The decision created quite a stir and elicited letters of complaint from a number of Friends, from one of the Monthly Meetings of Friends and from Anti-Slavery societies. The Central Relief Committee responded by bringing the matter to its meeting on 22nd April 1847 following which a statement was issued to the effect that while the committee did not wish to undermine the anti-slavery movement in any way, it did not feel that there was any cause to refuse these donations.

Another donation was not received so warmly. In the mid 19th century there was a wide gulf between what was considered to be proper activities by Friends and what was accepted by society at large. Friends were discouraged from engaging in any activity that was purely for entertainment, these being considered to be "inconsistent with the gravity and sobriety required of professors of Christianity", or even to be "nurseries of vice and immorality". As a result, when an exhibition was held in the Queen's Theatre, London which raised £70 towards the relief fund, the Central Relief Committee, to the approval of Friends at large, refused to accept the donation.

# CHAPTER SEVEN:

# PUBLICITY AND PUBLICATIONS

From the time of their inception the Quaker famine relief committees were adept publishing information as a means of keeping the famine in the minds of potential subscribers. As we have seen the first publications were the addresses to members of the Society of Friends and these were followed with a quick succession of publications in the early months of 1847. At the beginning of January the Dublin committee decided to print extracts of correspondence which gave details of the appalling state of the country and this included letters from William Forster on his journey in the west. The effects of these extracts would have been significant, bringing first hand accounts from a reliable witness painting bleak pictures of the starvation and misery which he encountered. The accounts also showed how assistance was being given by the party of Quakers as they progressed on their tour. Other correspondence which was included came from the committee's corresponding members in Cork, Limerick, Waterford and Clonmel and would have covered districts not visited by William Forster's party.

Some 7,000 copies of the this first extract from correspondence were printed, 1,500 of which were sent to London, while arrangements were made to sell copies through booksellers. As soon as this volume was published the Central Relief Committee began to plan a second volume containing further accounts of the distress and the measures which were being taken to relieve it. This was published in March 1847 with a print run of 5,000.

At the same time the London committee was publishing similar material. In January extracts were published from the report of James H. Tuke describing his experiences while accompanying William Forster in the previous month. This was followed by two further volumes, one from a report by W. D. Sims at the turn of the year and the other from William Edward Forster. Later, in April 1847, the committee published a further account of a tour in the west of Ireland, this time by R. Barclay Fox. The London committee also published early in 1847 reports of its proceedings stating the amounts of its receipts and disbursements and including an account of shipments of food from Liverpool.

The third volume to be published by the Dublin committee came in April 1847 when extracts of American correspondence were printed to demonstrate the extensive assistance which was being supplied from that quarter.

After this there was a lull in the publications by the committees, though individual Quakers published their own accounts. William Bennett produced a report of his visit during March 1847 when, as we shall see, he was distributing seeds. Like many of the other writers he included vivid accounts of the misery which he saw:

> We entered a cabin. Stretched in one dark corner, scarcely visible, from the smoke and rags that covered them, were three children huddled together, lying there *because they were too weak to rise*, pale and ghastly, their little limbs - on removing a portion of the filthy covering - perfectly emaciated, eyes sunk, voice gone, and evidently in the last stage of actual starvation. ... Many cases were widows whose husbands had recently been taken off by the fever, and their only pittance, obtained from the public works, entirely cut off.

As we have seen, James Hack Tuke wrote an account of his visit in the autumn of 1847, though this ran into problems when a landowner in Co. Mayo claimed that Tuke had misrepresented him in his account so that publication was suspended until a month or so later, in February 1848. Jonathan Pim published his own views on the land system in Ireland and the committees used these publications in its lobbying for political change.

The Central Relief Committee published an interim report in June 1848 giving an account of work undertaken to date and setting out its accounts. It was made clear in this publication that a more detailed account would be presented once the task was completed.

A year later the committee published an address to the public, following extensive consultations with the various Friends who were involved in the relief efforts, including the auxiliary committees. This reviewed the work undertaken by the committees over the previous two and a half years and came to the conclusion that the distress caused by the famine was so great as to be beyond the scope of such measures. Instead, fundamental changes were called for through such statements as "our paramount want is not money; it is the removal of those legal difficulties which prevent the capital of Ireland from being applied to the improved cultivation of the soil, and thus supporting its poor by the wages of honest and useful labour". This was to be done by restructuring the land law in Ireland and even before the address was published the first of the changes had been made.

Through this succession of publications, particularly those of the early months of the crisis, the committees increased public awareness of the problem and this helped to solicit subscriptions. Later publications managed to achieve changes in government attitudes and policies to some extent in the short term and in the longer term they helped to set in motion the overhaul of the land system.

This is to jump ahead, however. The setting up of an efficient organisation, the gathering of information and the raising of funds were all essential to the purpose of relieving distress, but they did nothing in themselves to help relieve the hunger. We should now look at the actual means of relief which were offered at various stages of the famine.

# CHAPTER EIGHT:

# SOUP KITCHENS

The most obvious way of helping those who were starving was to establish places from which food could be distributed and the most efficient way of distributing food was in the form of soup. Soup kitchens had been used for relief of distress on previous occasions in both Ireland and Great Britain, as early as the famine in Ireland in 1739-41. It was a constant problem in relief works that whatever was given to the destitute would be sold or pawned but pre-cooked food had no significant resale value and was therefore a reliable way of ensuring that relief was effective. During shortages it also removed the need for the recipient to have to cook the food using scarce or expensive fuel and, particularly in the worst-hit parts of Ireland, it got over the problem of the lack of any tradition of cooking foods other than the potato.

The first soup kitchens opened by Quakers were those which were run by local Friends meetings or individuals. By November 1846 Friends had opened soup shops in Clonmel, Limerick, Youghal and Waterford and others followed all around the country. In Waterford the operation of the soup kitchen got under way on 21st November and offered soup to the needy four times a week. Recipients were vetted before they could receive soup and this was done by two members of the committee who visited the applicants and assessed their need. Within a few days some 180 cases had been approved for relief and it was anticipated that this would increase to 500 or 600 within a fortnight. The relief offered consisted of a quart of soup and a half pound of bread, and this cost the committee two-pence farthing. On this basis, the operation of the soup kitchen cost Waterford Friends some £6.75p per week, or, at today's prices, about £370.

In January 1847 a soup-shop was opened by the Central Relief Committee in Charles Street, off Ormond Quay in Dublin. While Dublin was not so badly hit as the west, it had its share of hardship and had a definite need of relief measures. The other purpose of this soup kitchen was as a model for other establishments and the experience gained in the committee's own soup kitchen would be invaluable when they came to advise others who were establishing them elsewhere.

The soup kitchen in Charles Street was operated by a subcommittee of the Central Relief Committee with its members operating on a rota system, distributing the soup twice each day, six days a week from 7.30 to 9 am and 12 to 3 pm. At its peak the establishment dispensed an average of 1,000 quarts of soup each day, or well over a tonne, though the boiler was capable of producing nearly two and a half times that much. Soup was not given away but sold at the modest price of a penny a quart and, if bread were included the price would be one and a half pence. The system allowed for others to become involved in relief as tickets could be bought by anyone who wished to distribute them to the poor.

One of the most important lessons learned from the operation of the Charles Street soup kitchen was the optimum composition of the soup. A criticism of many soup establishments was that the liquid diet or the unwholesome food contained in it resulted in dysentery and this factor was brought to the committee's notice by William Forster during his tour in the west. In order to prevent this the Charles Street kitchen introduced cooked rice into the recipe in March 1847.

This soup kitchen operated for just six months until July 1847, by which time government relief schemes had changed and had largely rendered the operation unnecessary. During its operation it had dispensed more than 100,000 quarts, or more than 120 tonnes of soup and rice. The Waterford soup kitchen closed in June 1847.

The system used for cooking the soup involved an 80 gallon boiler which produced steam. The steam was carried through pipes into three wooden vats, each with a capacity of 200 gallons. The ingredients were put into the vats and cooked by the steam from the pipes. This system can be seen clearly in the well-known illustration of the soup kitchen in Cork which appeared in the *Illustrated London News* in January 1847. At that time Charles Street was mainly occupied by metal workers and metal merchants and the soup shop took its heat from the furnace in the adjacent premises of an iron worker.

*Quaker Soup Kitchen at Cork, January 1847*

The first major shipment of supplies received from Great Britain in February and March 1847 included a consignment of soup boilers. These were landed at various places along the west coast, the largest number, ten, going to Killybegs. The supply of boilers was greatly enhanced by the donation of no less than fifty-six of them from the Quaker iron manufacturers, Abraham and Alfred Darby of the Coalbrookdale Iron Company.

Over the first six months or so of 1847 the committee tried to encourage the setting up of soup shops around the country through the grant of money and of boilers. One example was at Templecrone, Co. Donegal, and here four soup boilers were in operation, being used twice a day to give out some 600 gallons of soup at a cost to the local organisers of £2 10s. As late as August 1847, several months after the government had decided to establish soup kitchens, this one still provided the only form of relief available in the parish and was insufficient for their needs. This operation was aided by the Central Relief Committee which granted a ton of rice, three tons of Indian meal, five quarters of peas and a ton of biscuits in mid July. Over the period of the famine the committee supplied almost three hundred soup boilers to twenty-seven of the thirty-two counties.

# CHAPTER NINE:
# DISTRIBUTION OF RELIEF

Soup kitchens are better suited to urban areas than the open countryside because of the numbers of portions which they can dispense in a day. Apart from this means of feeding the hungry Quakers were distributing food relief to local relief committees. From the outset the Central Relief Committee recognised that the distribution of relief to the worst-hit areas would be difficult as there were few Quakers living in these areas and often there were few others who could handle relief measures locally.

The subcommittee set up in November 1846 to decide on the best mode of relief concluded that the task would need to be pursued with great caution if the resources of the committee were not to be quickly used up. The best means were considered to be through encouraging local residents to become involved in the distribution of relief and by this method, people of all backgrounds and religious persuasions would dispense the relief provided by the Quaker committees. Care would also be necessary to ensure that the committee did not waste its resources in the duplication of work being carried out by other associations or the government. It was also thought expedient not to lay down strict procedures at the outset, presumably to allow the committee to learn by experience.

To prevent abuses and ensure that as high a proportion as possible of the funds was used for the purpose for which it was intended, a questionnaire was devised which each applicant for a grant had to complete. Apart from the obvious questions concerning location, extent of the area, numbers of people in distress, there were questions about the numbers of able bodied labourers, the presence of any fisheries, the amount of planting taking place, the amount of relief funds already subscribed locally, prices locally of various provisions, quantity of provisions in storage locally, presence of soup-shops, name of referee, and so forth.

Whenever the applicant for relief was not already known to the Committee enquiries were made as to the character and reliability of the person before any grants were made. If, after a grant had issued the committee was not happy with the way in which it had been used the matter could be investigated by one of the Friends visiting the area - as when Richard D.

Webb visited Erris to investigate claims of misappropriation of relief funds, thankfully finding no evidence for the claim. To minimise the chance of funds going astray the committee tended to make only small grants in the first instance, generally around ten to twenty pounds. If this was used to their satisfaction they would then make a further grant. The committee recognised that these repeated grants increased the workload to an already overburdened workforce but felt that it provided a worthwhile check.

A large proportion of the relief available through the committee was in the form of food rather than money and this brought several difficulties. In the first instance the committee was aware of the damage that could be caused to local trade by undercutting it through the distribution of food cheaper than it could be bought locally. To overcome this it was decided where possible to concentrate on commodities which were not normally available locally so that there was no local trade to undermine. Rice was distributed in large quantities for this reason and because it did not lead to the dysentery that was resulting from other foods. What effect this had indirectly on local trade through substitution for commodities such as flour is not recorded.

In December 1846 the London committee brought up the possibility of shipping food to ports in the west of Ireland. Conscious of the need to avoid undermining local trade enquiries were made in the western ports of Sligo, Galway and Westport as to the probable stocks of corn in those places and their expected imports. In January enquiries were complete and the committee wrote to London with a view to purchasing supplies of peas, rice and other produce which was not normally traded in the west and which would be suitable for soup.

Also in December 1846, reports reached the committee that the state of the people of Skibbereen in west Cork was particularly bad. The response was to request the committee's Cork correspondents to investigate and, if possible, visit the village. Three Cork Friends, William Harvey, Joshua G. Beale and Ebenezer Pike duly set out while other Cork Quakers set about raising a local subscription. The sum of £54 was collected and together with £300 from the Central Relief Committee it was used to help the destitute in Skibbereen and a further £500 was sent from the Central Relief Committee a few weeks later. It was this initial involvement which led to the setting up of a relief committee in Cork and, subsequently, the four auxiliary committees in Munster. Early in the following month the Poor Relief Committee of Quakers in Limerick sought financial assistance to help the destitute poor of that city. In granting £100 the Central Relief Committee enquired of Limerick Friends whether there was any general effort by the inhabitants of the city to relieve distress.

Early in February 1847 the London committee wrote to the Central Relief Committee to suggest that the amount of relief being offered should be increased and that it intended to purchase meal and ship it to some of the ports in the west. To this end the London committee sought the assistance of the government and was granted the use of two steamships for the purpose.

*Famine victims watching the arrival of a relief ship, January, 1847*

The two ships, *Albert and Scourge* left Liverpool in February 1847 and landed supplies in various western ports including Dunfanaghy, Belmullet, Westport and Clifden. The food carried included peas, rice, Indian meal, biscuit and American beef with a total value of more than £10,000, the cost of this exercise being raised partly in Liverpool and partly from the London committee. While the project was a general success it was not without problems, particularly due to the lack of any suitable local people to take charge of the supplies and lack of adequate storage facilities.

In the spring of 1847 the government changed its policy in relation to the provision of relief to the destitute. While the main form of government aid had been through relief works such as the building of roads now these works were to be closed and food would be available to those who needed it without having to be admitted to the poor houses. In essence, the government was to adopt the concept of the soup kitchen as a temporary measure, with the soup being provided by the poor law unions. While this system would cut out many of the problems experienced with the relief works, it was not going to be able to solve them entirely.

The Central Relief Committee was particularly concerned that the closure of the relief works would take place much quicker than the soup kitchens could be established and that there would be a considerable period when there would be less relief available. In a bid to minimise the effects of this hiatus the committee decided to step up its relief operations. Two of the committee met with Sir John Burgoyne, head of the government commissariat, to discuss the possibilities of getting information from the inspectors of the poor law unions regarding the extent of the destitution in their areas and the probable cost of supplying relief. Sir John agreed to this and sent a circular letter drafted by the committee to all inspectors of the poor law unions in Connaught and the western counties of Munster and Ulster.

While waiting for a reply to this circular, the committee began to consider what its role might be once the government soup kitchens came into operation and possibilities such as provision of industrial employment, cultivation of flax, encouragement of fisheries were considered. In April 1847 the committee noted that £25,000 had been expended and £50,000 remained, including the value of shipments of food. It seemed likely that the ensuing three or four weeks would be likely to be a period of particular pressure due to the reduction in the numbers of labourers on the relief works and the cessation in the work of many local relief committees. The plight of many tradesmen and artisans was also noted, as the entire economy of the country was being severely affected by the famine. While it seemed to be a worthwhile exercise to become involved in the provision of employment in industry, fisheries etc., the committee did not think that this was the right time. So long as there was a strong need for the feeding of the hungry and the clothing of the naked other forms of relief were not to be considered.

When the reply to the circular to the poor law unions arrived the committee was shocked to discover the extent of the destitution which extended through the western part of the country. At the same time the government replied to the committee that it was not prepared to use government funds to match the committee's for the supply of food. The result of these two factors brought the committee to the conclusion that the funds required for so large a project as feeding the people would be far beyond the means of the Quaker relief committees and .his plan was dropped.

In May the Central Relief Committee met with members of the auxiliary committees and several other Quakers. This meeting was told of the amounts of relief granted and food received by ship. Several of those present believed that the distress was still on the increase but the scale of the grants which had been made to date during the changeover in government relief measures was such that the committee had to write to the auxiliary committees in Cork and Limerick to ask them to moderate the amount of relief being dispensed.

By September, the whole pattern of relief measures in Ireland had changed. The new harvest was not struck by the potato blight, but as very little had been planted the harvest was small and starvation continued. Distress was now occurring as a result of the discontinuation of the temporary relief measures which had been introduced in the spring. The Central Relief Committee had some difficult decisions to make as the destitute continued to die. After a great deal of thought the committee came to the conclusion that its funds would be inadequate to warrant attempting any comprehensive system of relief aimed at those for whom relief was supposed to be available from government sources. It was also considered that temporary assistance would retard the carrying of the new poor law into operation. In these circumstances the committee decided that it would discontinue the issue of food except to those for whom the stringencies of the legal measures for relief would exclude from care. In place of food relief it was decided that more effort would be put into the promotion of industry and other programmes for the longer term improvement of the people.

At the end of January 1848 the committee decided to write to the auxiliary committees to ask if they proposed organising their soup kitchens during this winter. Information was also sought from the non-Quaker local relief committees in various towns in the west as to whether there had been an efficient distribution of soup in the previous winter and whether it was thought desirable to attempt this again this year. Several replies were received to this request and none of them recommended the re-establishment of soup kitchens, a view that concurred with that of the committee. There had been a suggestion that the Charles Street soup shop should be reopened to sell cooked rice, oatmeal or Indian meal stirabout at a low price however the soup committee, after careful consideration, decided that it would not be advisable and that it should dispose of the premises.

In March 1848 the Clonmel auxiliary committee, which had not been dispensing aid for some time, recommenced its work with a grant of £200 and fifty bags of rice from the Central Relief Committee. A month later the Limerick committee was almost out of supplies and was given £100 and in June £500 was given to the Cork committee with a request that distribution should henceforth be made with a sparing hand, to which the reply was that this amount should last until the arrival of the new harvest.

The Limerick committee was concerned that there was a loss of momentum and direction in the operations and at the beginning of May it called a conference of Quakers from Limerick and other parts of Munster to discuss future policy. Those present were united in their opinion that in future the energies of the committees should be directed towards the encouragement of industry and that further grants of money, food and clothing should be limited as far as was possible. It was recognised, however, that there was still a great deal of destitution that was not being reached by the government measures, especially in cases of sickness and convalescence and it was agreed that aid would continue in those cases, keeping within prudent limits for a limited period of three months. After that the new harvest would have been brought in and the crisis would be over, or so it was hoped.

The distribution of food, clothing and money by the various committees came to a virtual stop in the summer of 1848 as the policy came to concentrate more on relief efforts with longer term benefits.

The potato crop failed again in the autumn of 1848, resulting in a particularly severe episode of the famine. The long period of exertion had exacted a toll on the resources and energies of the members of the Society of Friends which, after all, was a comparatively small body. For this reason the direct relief through the distribution of food, money and clothing all but ceased in this period. In June 1849, when the crisis was at its worst, the Central Relief Committee received an enquiry from the Lord Lieutenant enquiring about its intentions for restarting relief and offering a donation of £100. The committee discussed the idea at length, but concluded that it was not possible to recommence any system of almsgiving. A tactful reply was sent to inform the Lord Lieutenant that the committee appreciated his confidence in their abilities, but declining the offer.

Even as this correspondence was under way the London committee was considering how it would dispose of the balance of the funds which it held. No decision was made in June on this issue, but by July there were suggestions that a new impetus for the giving of direct relief was needed. In mid July the London committee wrote to the Central Relief Committee referring to reports of severe distress in the south and west pending the arrival of the harvest and that the holders of small portions of land were in a state of great suffering and excluded from the provisions of the law which offered relief. This was a reference to the so-called Gregory clause in the poor law which excluded anyone holding more than a quarter acre of land from benefiting from the government system of relief from the poor houses. At the same time as the London committee wrote letters were arriving from various people who had received assistance in the past and from the auxiliary committees urging that some new efforts be made. As a result the London committee decided to hand £2,000 over to the Dublin committee for use in providing direct relief.

In the light of these pressures the Central Relief Committee decided to recommence relief operations, but this time the aid offered would not be gratuitous. No grants of money would be made unless there was an understanding that it should be employed in the promotion of agricultural labour. As the funds were extremely limited it was now considered to be wasteful to give grants that would have no long term benefit. In effect, payments would be made on the basis that the recipient would use it to improve his own land for future planting. Projects such as returning waste land to cultivation, subsoiling, draining, levelling fences, clearing stones off land and so forth were to be encouraged and where this was not possible funds could be used for the cutting of turf for fuel. There was to be a limit of £2 to £3 expenditure on a single smallholding in order to make the funds go further and each recipient would be expected to state who had been assisted and what works had been done. Over the next few weeks varying amounts were granted as relief, ranging from £10 to £470 in total per week and once the harvest came in it was possible to discontinue this short burst of aid.

The distribution of food, clothes and money during the famine had been at its most successful in the winter of 1846-47. As the famine progressed, however, this highly intense form of relief began to take its toll on the resources and energies of those involved in the Quaker committees. The committee members had become involved in a project which was likely to last for ten months or so, but in the event it kept going for four times that long.

While the Quaker distribution of relief only scratched the surface of the problem it was successful in a number of ways. Above all, it was a precondition of all relief offered by the Quakers that it would be offered regardless of religious persuasion and that the relief would have no strings attached. The committee believed that in this it was successful. The remoteness of the committee from the worst devastation made it inevitable that some abuse would occur such as when a magistrate was alleged to have misappropriated grants of food in Ballina. Is seems, however, that abuses of any kind, whether through theft of food or transgression of the ban on proselytising, were kept to a minimum.

# CHAPTER TEN:

# CLOTHING THE NAKED

In the early stages of a food shortage the hungry tend to pawn clothing to get small amounts of cash to buy food. As time passes the lack of adequate clothing results in suffering and deaths. The winter of 1846-47 was a particularly bad one so that the shortage of clothing became a severe problem as William Forster found during his tour, and there was concern that any clothing which might be distributed would end up in the pawnshop. William E. Forster spoke to pawnbrokers in Galway on this issue and concluded that this problem could be solved by stamping the clothing in some distinctive way.

Early in January 1847 the Central Relief Committee received a request for assistance from a voluntary organisation in Mountmellick known as the Dorcas Institute for Clothing the Poor of the Town. At this time the committee was only just starting to set up its relief organisation and felt that supplying clothing was not in its remit at that time, so the request was refused.

When the committee did become involved in clothing a few weeks later, at the end of January 1847, it was due to English initiative. Women Quakers in London were fired with enthusiasm by the reports from William Forster's tour and issued an appeal to the women of England to set up associations to make, prepare and collect clothes to send to the Central Relief Committee. Such was the desire to be able to help that transport of the bales of clothing made up by these committees was provided free of charge by railway companies in England and brought to Ireland without charge by Irish steampacket companies.

The large quantity of clothing arriving was too much for the Central Relief Committee to handle unaided and the decision was taken to set up a subcommittee to take charge of consignments of clothing and to communicate with a women's committee which was being formed at that time in Dublin. This subcommittee was to be comprised of Joshua Harvey, MD, Richard Allen, William Doyle, Joseph Allen (Secretary) and Henry Perry (Treasurer) and it was given fairly wide ranging authority including permission to take on premises and employ staff. A warehouse was taken at 20 Upper Bridge Street, Dublin, and staff were employed. An address to the people of England was drafted urging people to examine their wardrobes for clothing no longer required and requesting manufacturers to send any clothing which was not of quality suitable for sale. A form was printed on which applications could be made for clothing grants, on similar lines to that produced for applications for food relief.

In February William Forster wrote from his tour of the west with a proposal to supply shoes for labourers at one third of cost. This idea was to be discussed with the government, but seems to have come to nothing at this stage. Shoes were supplied by the subcommittee, however, as part of the normal relief measures and these were sold to labourers at cost on the basis of small weekly payments.

By April 1847 the government had announced its new temporary measures for relief, which would include soup supplied to people who were not inmates of the poor houses. The committee realised that this would still leave people without adequate clothing and shoes, so that clothing could become a major part of the committee's relief operations. Reports were coming in at this time that there was a severe shortage of proper clothing among the destitute and the number of applications for

*Form of application*

TO CLOTHING COMMITTEE.

No. _____ Mo. _____

I apply for _____

_____

for _____

of _____

whom I have visited in ____ dwelling ____

VISITOR.

*Application form for clothing grants.*

assistance was greatly increased. As a result, the clothing subcommittee had to employ an additional clerk, bringing its staff to a total of three clerks, one packer and a boy, while further assistance was necessary at particularly busy times. Most of the ready-made clothing received from England had been allocated by this time and the subcommittee had purchased large amounts of worsted and cotton for knitting, together with calicos, cords, flannels, drab fustian for jackets, cotton sheets, rugs and leather. A total of 150 packages of clothing had been received from England together with £575 in cash, but nevertheless funds were exhausted. In the circumstances the subcommittee was unsure whether it could continue its operations, despite the number of applications for relief having reached fifty in one week, the highest demand ever. The Central Relief Committee agreed to underwrite the cost of the clothing subcommittee for the time being, and

Letter from J. J. Fisher regarding a donation to provide clothing in Scariff.

shortly afterwards advanced £500 for the purpose. The subcommittee then wrote to the London committee to explain the circumstances in an effort to increase the amount of clothing to be sent.

By May, the "Ladies Irish Clothing Society" in England had collected some £4,700 from individuals and committees throughout England and had forwarded 86 bales of clothing to various parts of Ireland. This society was mainly composed of Quakers and met at least once a week for about five hours in order to get through its business. In an attempt to encourage employment in Ireland it tried to concentrate on fabrics rather than ready-made clothing and after a time this society was offered assistance from the British Association on the condition that it should extend its operations to the destitute people of Scotland who were also suffering from the famine, though not on so large a scale.

By the middle of July the worst of the clothing crisis was over and the subcommittee began to think about winding up its operations. The donations had slowed down to a trickle and the cost of retaining the employees was very large in comparison with the work on hand. Accordingly, the decision was taken to wind up the clothing subcommittee and to notify the London Ladies Committee who had been supplying so much of the clothing donations. The organisation finally closed at the end of August. During the seven months or so of its existence the subcommittee had received and distributed 210 packages of clothing and more than £1,800 in cash, over and above the £500 from the main committee. This had been distributed in a total of 668 grants to the most distressed districts. Among the towns which had contributed to this scheme London provided two thirds of the cash donations, with more than £1,200. Of the other fifty towns or so, Leeds stands out as the largest contributor of both money (£354) and clothing (48 bales, or almost a quarter of the total). The grants of clothing and money for clothing went to every county in Ireland, with the smallest amount to Louth (1 bale) and the largest to Cork (70 bales) followed by Galway, Tipperary, Offaly and Roscommon with more than 40 bales each.

During this time the Central Relief Committee was assisting the provision of clothing by other committees such as the Limerick auxiliary committee which was granted £100 for its clothing committee in June 1847.

No sooner had the clothing subcommittee finished its work than the problem surfaced again and consideration was given to the setting up of a new clothing subcommittee. It was not until the end of October, however, that moves were made and a subcommittee was set up to assess the need for premises. It was decided that the previous warehouse in Upper Bridge Street was inadequate and that an alternative must be found. James Perry and Nathaniel Williams inspected a possible alternative at Cole Alley, but did not think that it would be suitable. Before long premises were found on Merchants Quay which were leased from the representatives of Henry Cochrane for six months at £50 per month, with a similar rent to apply if the period was extended.

Once a warehouse had been found a clothing committee was appointed, comprised of James Perry, Joseph Allen and Thomas Pim junior with terms of reference to provide all clothing materials, have clothing made up where necessary, oversee the management of the warehouse and have clothing forwarded. This committee was authorised to take on staff and set up a subcommittee to decide on applications for relief. The recommendation to the clothing committee was that it should concentrate on materials for clothing rather than ready-made so as to encourage employment. The materials should include, in particular, flannels, grey calicoes, blue prints, corduroy, guernsey shirts, bed rugs, cotton shirts and leather for shoes and as far as was possible the cost of the materials should be repaid out of the earnings of the recipients.

Over the period of its operations the second clothing committee dispensed grants worth more than £6,300, of which some £1,300 or so was repaid, leaving a net cost of almost £5,000. Over and above this was the value of some clothes received from America. The committee made a total of 612 grants, once again to every county, Louth again receiving one bale while Galway received 52 and Roscommon, Cork, Donegal, Tipperary and Fermanagh got more than 35 each. There is a suggestion that some of the operations of the clothing committee were liable to abuse, but the nature and extent of this abuse is not certain and it does not seem to have been on a significant scale.

The Waterford auxiliary committee was given permission to allocate £300 for clothing purposes in mid September 1847, a further £300 was sent in

February 1848 and in total Waterford received £741 from the Central Relief Committee, £380 of which was repaid. The Cork subcommittee and the Ladies Relief Association of Dublin each also received small sums towards clothing.

# CHAPTER ELEVEN:
# SEED DISTRIBUTION

In March 1847, while William Forster was still touring the west, a London Quaker, William Bennett, arrived in Ireland intending to acquire seeds for green crops with his own funds and some donations. He announced his intention to distribute these seeds among small farmers in remote parts of Ireland to help in the longer term to provide food for the following season. The Central Relief Committee was not convinced that this was a worthwhile tactic at this stage and tried to discourage him, but he was not to be swayed. From W. Drummond & Sons, the Dublin seed merchants, he acquired some two hundredweight of turnip, carrot and mangel-wurzel seed, with small quantities of other varieties in addition and he set off by coach to Boyle, Co. Roscommon. He distributed his seeds in Mayo and Donegal by handing over quantities to responsible people locally for distribution to the needy and he was also able to distribute some money from the Ladies Committee in London for the support of charitable organisations.

William Bennett published his experiences in a booklet entitled *Six Weeks in Ireland,* in which he described the horrendous scenes of starvation and misery which he had seen. The seeds which he had distributed were not always planted properly and later visitors in the west reported seeing turnips planted far too close so that they could not develop properly, as the growers had no experience of this type of crop. However, reports concluded that even planted in this way the turnips helped to provide food to save lives.

In March 1847, while William Bennett was on his tour, the Central Relief Committee was approached by the Cork and Waterford auxiliary committees as they were concerned at the neglect of tillage around the country due to the inability of smallholders to purchase seeds. The Waterford auxiliary committee had made a grant of seeds to some freehold cottiers in the Forth mountains, but the Central Relief Committee felt that it was not safe to offer this assistance to smallholders except in certain circumstances. The reason for this was that the famine had left smallholders without the means to pay their rents and many of them were badly in arrears. Debts such as these would often result in the confiscation of property and the committee felt that seeds distributed to smallholders would be of no ultimate use as the crops would be seized by the landlords.

Towards the end of May 1847 the Central Relief Committee was granted some 40,000 lbs. (18 tonnes) of green-crop seeds by the government. The initiative for this came from Sir Randolph Routh, Commissary-General, who found that these seeds were in the hands of the government and were unlikely to be sold in that season as it was already late for sowing. Rather than see the seeds unused, he decided to hand them over to the committee. The committee, in turn, appointed William Todhunter to look after the distribution and he managed this with the aid of the postal system together with free transport being donated by a coach company and a steampacket company. Seed grants were made to more than 40,000 smallholders in seventeen counties and as a result more than 9,600 acres were sown with a probable yield of more than 190,000 tons of turnips.

In February 1848 the distribution of seeds came before the committee again for discussion. The British Association had decided to decline to get involved in this measure due to a shortage of funds, but the Central Relief Committee felt that it had the resources and that in the light of the previous year this would be a useful exercise. It was decided to appoint a subcommittee to distribute seeds, with a budget of £5,000 and this year the scale of the exercise was increased and more than 130,000 lbs. (59 tonnes) of seeds were purchased and distributed. It was estimated that as a result more than 32,000 acres were sown and this would have supplied food to nearly 150,000 people. A total of twenty four counties received seeds in the 1848 distribution and these were mainly turnip with some carrot, parsnip and cabbage. Almost half of the turnip seeds went to Mayo, with Galway and Cork also receiving large amounts. In all, the purchase and distribution of seeds in 1848 cost the committee about £6,300.

# CHAPTER TWELVE:

# FISHERIES

During his tour in the west in January 1847, William Forster visited the Claddagh in Galway. Here he found that the community of fishermen and their families, amounting to about 4,000 people, was in a "fearful depth of misery". A curious effect of the famine was a decrease in the consumption of fish, as fish tended to be eaten with potatoes and this habit was strong enough that without potatoes fewer people ate fish. In addition, the fish were in short supply in the coastal waters at this time and as a result of these circumstances many of the fishermen had pawned most of their possessions, including their nets and tackle. William Forster's son, William Edward Forster, confirmed this with the pawnbrokers, finding that two or three of the brokers had in pledge at least a thousand pounds worth of equipment which they did not see would ever be redeemed. This immediate problem was overcome through the making of grants to the fishermen to redeem their nets and tackle from pawn and to repair their boats ready for when the herring should return.

During the spring of 1847 the Waterford auxiliary committee became involved in fisheries when they provided funds for the promotion of coastal fishery at Ballinacourty near Dungarvan. This project did not succeed and the balance of the funds was returned to the committee. At the same time, the Waterford committee received a request for assistance from the vicar of the parish of Ring, Rev. James Alcock, who was concerned that the fishermen in his locality were destitute despite having the potential to support themselves. They were unable to fish as their boats needed to be repaired, their oars had been burned as fuel and their clothes, furniture and fishing gear had been pawned. The committee reacted by supplying food and the first instalment of a series of loans through which the nets and tackle could be redeemed and the boats made ready for the sea. The result was that over time the fishing community at Ring became self-supporting. Not content with this achievement, Rev. Alcock continued his work to improve the fisheries with financial assistance from the committee. This included the building of two boats of a new design which would be better suited to the local conditions than either the smaller boats being used by the fishermen or the more expensive and more unwieldy Hookers. He also put a great deal of energy into a campaign for the relaxation of a law which restricted the use of trammel nets to night time only and which was severely curtailing the operations of the fishermen. Most of the loans advanced to the fishermen were repaid to the committee from the renewed earnings.

A second enterprise which was set up alongside the fisheries at Ring was a fish-curing plant. This was set up by two Scottish entrepreneurs who had visited the district and seen the potential for such a project. The committee advanced them £100 towards the enterprise and it was duly set up at Helvick Head and operated successfully for a time, aided by a further £100 from the committee. However, the two proprietors also became involved in farm management even though they had no knowledge of agriculture and they ran into problems which forced the closure of the curing plant and their return to Scotland.

Assisting fisheries would seem to be an obvious means of providing relief during a famine as it would give employment while also increasing the supply of food. This fact was not lost on the Commissioner for the Fishery Department of the Board of Works, William T. Mulvany, who approached the Central Relief Committee in May 1847 with a suggestion that the committee should allocate funds for this purpose. His proposal was similar to what had already taken place in the Claddagh and Ring, namely the advancement of money to suitable people who could allocate it as loans to fishermen for the provision of fishing gear and the repair of boats. What had led to his approach was the government proposal to establish fish curing stations on the west coast which highlighted the poor state of the fishermen as fish curing was of no use if there was no equipment with which to catch the fish in the first place. After consultations with the Chairman of the Government Relief Commission and the Commander of the coastguard and after seeking comment from coastguard officers around the country, the committee decided to allocate £250 to the coastguard on the basis that the coastguard officers were in the best position to administer loans to the fishermen. It was William Mulvany himself who pointed out how bizarre it was for a public body to be coming to a benevolent organisation seeking assistance and, indeed, this was not the only occasion during the famine that the committee agreed to advance funds to a public body. In the end, the offer was not taken up by the coastguard.

## Information obtained by the Relief Committee of the Society of Friends, Limerick, relative to Curing Fish, so successfully practised in the County Waterford.

### METHOD OF CURING HADDOCK.

*At Ring, Helvick, near Dungarvan.*

OPEN and clean the fish carefully, cut off the head, immerse them in a tub of water, and wash away all impurities. Then take and split the fish from end to end, leaving merely the skin, and wash in a clean water; put them in pickle for 30 minutes, then put them on rods in the smoking house; if the house be full of fish, 24 hours will suffice; if not full, a longer time will be required. Larger Haddock require to be left a longer time in the pickle.

Fish thus cured will keep 14 days. Should it be necessary to hold it a longer time, let it remain one hour in the pickle.

Hardwood, as Oak, Beech, Elm, Birch, is used for smoking—turf is added, should the fire become too great; but turf causes too much dust for general use. Pine wood imparts a bitter taste to the fish and is not approved of.

### TO SMOKE HERRINGS.

Pack them carefully in barrels, placing salt between every layer, till full; then fill with pickle to the top; let them remain thus three days; then take them out, and wash in fresh water, and hang them up by the gills in the smoking house.

Note—The Herrings may remain 12 months in the barrels, before smoking, without injury; but it will be necessary to steep them in *fresh water*, to remove some of the salt, should they be any length of time in pickle. The longer they have remained in the barrels the more steeping they will require.

Great care must be taken that the *fire* is not too hot, while the process of smoking goes on, as much injury may be caused in a very few minutes.—This is easily perceived by examining the Herrings from time to time, and if they become soft near the tails, or the fish rises from the bone, or they drop from the rods on which they are suspended, the fire should be *immediately* reduced.

### TO CURE COD, LING, HAKE, &c.

Open and clean the fish, cut off the head, and remove the backbone, to the lower extremity of the belly, then wash away all blood, &c., very carefully, continue the cut down to the tail, close by the remaining part of the backbone, in doing this you expose to view a blood-vessel, which should be carefully opened; then wash, and remove all the black lining of the stomach, and other impurities. Pickle for a week, and dry in the sun.

In Scotland large quantities of Haddock are cured, by cleaning and splitting as before described, and laying them on the rocks, near the water's edge, sprinkling with salt water, from time to time, till perfectly cured, and then dried—this is done without using any salt, except what is in the salt water.

The Smoking House at Helvick is 32 feet long, by 14, and about 30 feet in height, with beams across, at intervals of four feet, on which the rods are supported; the perpendicular distance between those beams is not more than 14 inches, that being more than the length of the largest Haddock. The first tier of beams commence about seven feet above the floor on which the fires are.

JOHN ABELL.
ISAAC W. UNTHANK.

Limerick, 3d Month 21st, 1848.

☞ Fishermen are recommended to have this information preserved, by pasting it in their houses.

*Handbill issued by the Limerick Auxiliary Committee with advice to fisherman on the curing of fish*

Later in 1847 the Central Relief Committee took the opportunity to become more heavily involved in the fisheries as it was seen that this presented great opportunities for the longer-term improvement of the country. In October 1847, the committee was approached by Thomas F. Eastwood who had conducted a simple fishery experiment at Ballinakill Bay, near Clifden and who asked the committee if it would agree to appoint him to manage a fishery station there as trustee of the committee. The committee allocated £300 to him for the purchase of boats, curraghs and equipment but the enterprise did not succeed and was shut down after a short period. Another project, at Achill Sound, was similarly unsuccessful and short-lived.

Another approach came from William T. Campbell of Belmullet, Co. Mayo, who proposed that the committee should assist him to establish a fishery there. As with the Ballinakill Bay project, it was agreed to allocate £300 to him for the fitting out of 15 fishing boats and 10 curraghs, to be repaid out of the earnings of the boats. A year later, at the end of 1849, the committee sent a delegation to inspect the fisheries at Belmullet. They found that W. T. Campbell had not been efficient in his management of the station, having spent too lavishly, failed to select crews carefully and had not kept a sufficiently close eye on the operations of boats, nor kept proper accounts. By contrast, it was found that another man nearby had been fishing more profitably, suggesting that Campbell's fishery had failed through mismanagement rather than poor location. The decision was taken to close the fishery at Belmullet and that the committee would not meet the outstanding debts of the venture as they had been incurred by William Campbell outside the terms of his agreement with the Central Relief Committee.

Charles Bushe of Castletown, Berehaven, Co. Cork similarly approached the committee in October 1847, through corresponding members, seeking assistance for fisheries there. In December he asked that a good sized cutter should be made available to assist the smaller fishing boats and the committee responded by leasing a trawler of 53 tons and named the *Erne*. The fishery at Castletown was put under the management of Wight Pike of Cork and a fish curing plant was established. A year later, the committee felt that this fishery did not seem worthwhile and that it should be closed. Joshua Fayle, the resident manager at the fishery, prepared a report in which he set down several problems with the operation of a fishery station here. The original location had been at Castletown but it had been transferred to Bere Island which was more suitable, but not perfect. Its particular problems were that it was 25 miles from the fishing ground during part of the season and this necessitated rowing out and back on every trip; there was no adequate supply of bait nearby and there was no source of suitable provisions for the boats. The shortage of bait was a problem which had been found elsewhere and resulted from local mussel beds being cleared out by people seeking food during the worst of the famine. Joshua Fayle put forward a number of suggestions for the improvement of the fishery at Bere Island, including the reseeding of the mussel beds to provide a source of bait and the supply of sea biscuit at a modest price to provision the boats. There were nine boats operating here with a total of 54 men and boys employed.

The committee reacted to this report by deciding to remove Wight Pike from his position as manager and appoint Joshua Fayle in his place at 20 shillings a week with permission to draw 25 shillings if necessary. A year later, it was reported that the fishery at Castletown was on the whole satisfactory and that the first £100 of the loan had been repaid to the committee. In February 1851 Joshua Fayle reported to the Central Relief Committee with the details of the quantities of fish which had been caught using the different methods. Of these, the Seine net was proving to be the most profitable and at the same time gave the most employment. Two Dublin fishermen had been engaged to manage two 12 ton boats with a view to giving instruction to the local fishermen and between all of the various improved methods which had been introduced the condition of the local people had been noticeably improved. The low price of fish was a continuing problem and militated against selling the fish to the Dublin market because of the high cost of transport over that distance.

After a further year, the committee had heard nothing more from Joshua Fayle and no reply had been received to a letter written to him so it was decided that someone should go to Castletown to investigate. Manliffe Barrington travelled from Dublin and found that the fishery consisted of a house, stores and yard at Castletown and a store and yard at Laurence's Cove, Bere Island. Joshua Fayle was living in the house and all of the boats were at Bere Island. Alarmingly, Manliffe Barrington found that

Joshua Fayle had not kept any proper account books during the entire time since he took over from Wight Pike, though he claimed that he had all of the necessary documents to enable him to set down the accounts if he were given time. He also stated that the committee had guaranteed him 25 shillings a week should his income from the fisheries not come to this amount and that although he had not worked at the fisheries since the previous November he felt entitled to this payment up to date on the grounds that he had been responsible for the property. While the boats were in reasonably good condition they were not sufficiently seaworthy to allow them to be brought to Dublin for sale and they would have to be sold locally. Joshua Fayle put forward the proposition that the property be sold to him, believing that his family would give him the means to purchase it. Investigations by Manliffe Barrington and his companion, Joshua E. Todhunter, showed that the fish were no longer present in the region of this fishery station in sufficient quantities to be commercially viable and, accordingly, the decision was taken to close the fishery at Castletown.

Some time after the *Erne* had taken up its station at Castletown it became evident that it was not of as much use as a backup to the smaller boats as had been anticipated. It was decided, therefore, to take it away from that fishery and employ it more efficiently in investigating the potential for fisheries in general off the west coast. It was generally believed that there were rich fishing grounds in various places if only the fishermen could be persuaded to make use of them but it soon became apparent that this was not the case. The *Erne* found that the available charts of the waters to the west of Ireland were not accurate, that the bottom of the sea was generally so rocky that it would cause severe damage to nets if trawling was attempted and that the amount of fish in the water was not great. In addition, the westerly winds ensured that the *Erne* was not able to remain in the open sea long enough to fish commercially. A great deal of investigation of the potential of the western waters for fishing was carried out by William Todhunter, a member of the Central Relief Committee, during a three month period spent on the *Erne*.

While the Central Relief Committee was engaged in these fisheries and a host of other projects, the London committee took on its own involvement with the fisheries. One of the first undertakings was the lobbying of the government in an attempt to have the charts of the coastal waters brought up to date and in this the committee succeeded and a new survey of the Irish fishing grounds was undertaken by the Royal Navy.

A more demanding task undertaken by the London committee was the improvement of the fishery at the Claddagh. The assistance given in January 1847 by William Forster had enabled the fishery to survive, but it was recognised at the time that a larger grant could have done so much more to improve the operations. An additional factor in favour of this proposal was that there was already a school of fisheries at the Claddagh that was run by the Dominican Order which could act as an intermediary and which could form the basis for improvements. In the spring of 1848 John Hodgkin of the London committee, acting in tandem with the Limerick auxiliary committee, began moves to improve the Claddagh fishery. A Cornish deep-sea fisherman, Captain Arthur Chard, was employed to teach modern methods to the Claddagh fishermen and he started by redeeming the nets and tackle from pawn once again.

*Letter from R. Barclay Fox of the London Committee relating to the employment of Captain Arthur Chard at the Claddagh.*

The next move was to establish a fish curing plant and after various problems a building was found and converted for use. The project never achieved the potential that was hoped for it for a number of reasons. Firstly, there was a language barrier, as the Claddagh people spoke no English. Secondly, the community in the Claddagh was extremely self-contained and did not respond well to outside influences, nor were they willing to change their old traditions lightly. They opposed the introduction of trawling, a problem that was exacerbated by the unsuitability of the boat which had been purchased for the purpose, the *Vivid*, acquired in Cornwall, the design and equipment of which was not well suited to the heavy conditions found off the Galway coast. In 1850, the London committee decided "to give up their attempts to induce the fishermen at the Claddagh to avail themselves of improved modes of fishing". They handed over the *Vivid* on loan to the Central Relief Committee and it was transferred to Castletown Berehaven. The loan was later changed to a gift and the *Vivid* remained at Bere Island until the closure of those fisheries.

In addition to these projects, the Central Relief Committee and its various associate committees made several other grants to aid fisheries. In June 1847 £50 was advanced for the assistance of the fishermen of Arklow, allowing 161 nets to be redeemed from pawn and more than 160 families were made self-sufficient. The value of the first night's catch exceeded the amount of the loan and within a week loans to these fishermen began to be repaid. Four months later all but three had been remitted to the committee, the three outstanding loans being due to the death of one fisherman, the destruction of another's nets and the delay in the third due to the cost of repairs to his boat. Loans were also extended to fishermen in Kingstown, Dunmore East, Cloyne and Ballycotton. This last named fishing community was also assisted by the Cork auxiliary committee and together with other grants it was possible for the men to return to fishing while an industrial enterprise was set up in which nets, fishermen's clothing and blankets were manufactured from hemp and other fibres. In November 1847 a loan of £150 was extended to Maurice O'Connell, MP, son of the late Daniel O'Connell, for the provision of boats, gear and nets to assist numerous unemployed fishermen in the vicinity of his house at Derrynane

Abbey, Co. Kerry. It was agreed that £300 would be allocated to him, though he only drew on £150 and this was repaid in August 1849.

Inland fisheries were not forgotten, and assistance was given to fishermen on Lough Neagh, beginning with a grant of £15 in the autumn of 1847 for the provision of nets and clothing. The law forbade fishing in Lough Neagh from October to mid February and this caused great hardship to the fishermen. While the law was not enforced in October and November of 1847 the magistrates and police began to keep a close watch in December and the fishermen found themselves without food or income. John Hodgkin of the London committee undertook to raise this matter with the authorities if it could be shown that the basis of the law was ill-founded.

The overall picture of the various fisheries supported by the Society of Friends does not look impressive. The schemes into which the most money was placed were by and large unsuccessful, and the longest-lived of them all, Castletown, was kept going beyond the point at which it was seen to be unprofitable merely because of the amount of money that had been invested in it. However, even the seemingly unsuccessful ventures succeeded in providing incomes for a considerable number of families through some of the worst periods of the famine and the overall cost to the committee per family helped per week would have been very much less than the cost of maintaining them through soup kitchens quite apart from the effects on the self-respect of the families. The schemes which are given the least space in the reports of the various committees are those in which the greatest ultimate benefit would have accrued, such as the Arklow and Ballycotton fisheries, where a small initial input led to a much longer term period of self-sufficiency. Of the major fishery projects of the Society of Friends, the most successful would seem to have been those at Ring, the ultimate credit for which must be given to their sponsor, Rev. James Alcock.

In addition to the fisheries which were assisted, both the Dublin and London committees lobbied the government for changes in the law relating to fisheries and, as noted, succeeded in getting new charts surveyed for the west coast fisheries. The esteem in which the government and its officials held the committees was illustrated by the approach for assistance from the Commissioner for the Fishery Department and also by the request which

# POLLEN FISHERY.

## LOUGH NEAGH.

The Commissioners acting in execution of an Act, made and passed in the 5th and 6th years of the Reign of Her present Majesty, entituled "An Act to regulate the Irish Fisheries," and two further Acts since passed amending the same, having had under consideration various applicacations to authorise the use of certain Nets for the taking of *Pollen*, have authorised and sanctioned, and do hereby authorise and sanction, that the said Fish called and known by the name of *Pollen*, may be fished for and taken in Lough Neagh during the Open Season, viz., from 12th day of February, to the 1st day of October in each year, *by Trammel or set Nets, composed of Thread or Yarn of a fine texture, being not less than ten hanks to the pound weight, doubled and twisted with a Mesh, in no place less than one inch from knot to knot,* and from the 15th day of May to the first day of the Close Time now fixed, viz., the 20th day of August, or hereafter to be appointed for the Salmon Fishery, *by draught Nets having a Mesh, in no place less than one inch from knot to knot.*

HARRY D JONES, } *Commissioners.*
W. T. MULVANY, }

*Dated at the Office of Public Works, Custom House, Dublin, this*

*Government handbill authorising Pollen fishing at Lough Neagh*

came from the Lord Lieutenant in December 1847, seeking an interview with the committee in relation to the fisheries. William Todhunter attended on behalf of the committee and was received by the Lord Lieutenant "with much kindness ... for upwards of an hour".

# CHAPTER THIRTEEN:

# AGRICULTURE

## Spade cultivation at Ballina

The traditional method of tilling the ground in Ireland amongst a large proportion of the smaller farmers was by spade cultivation, rather than the use of the plough. Many people had only a small plot of ground, amounting to an acre or so, on which they grew their potatoes and this was done by spade labour, but even on larger holdings the spade was used for a wide variety of crops. In February 1848 the County Surveyor for Mayo, Henry Brett, suggested that the committee should help the destitute farmers of Erris to cultivate their lands, but it was not possible for the committee to get involved in this proposal.

At the same time, a group of landowners in the vicinity of Ballina, Co. Mayo, led by George Vaughan Jackson, offered to let the Central Relief Committee have the use of a large amount of land free of rent for a single season. It was decided to take up this offer and some 550 Irish acres were selected with a view to cultivating it by means of the spade. The project involved more than thirty farms spread over a distance of fourteen miles by twelve miles on the Mayo/Sligo border. The soil was good but it had never been well cultivated and had lain idle for at least a year because of the famine and was not in a good state for the planting of green crops due to the heavy weed cover. More than a thousand people were taken on to work the scheme and they were to be paid by task-work, with the rates of pay somewhat above normal to allow for the poor condition of the workers following a period of starvation. Before long the project was costing £300 a week while sometimes reaching £400 or even £500 a week, mostly in wages, though there was also a significant cost for fertiliser. In order to avoid cornering the local market for fertilisers with this major undertaking the decision was taken to buy in fertiliser such as guano. The crops to be planted were to be predominantly turnip and other green crops, though for obvious reasons potatoes would not be included and in addition, some 75 acres of flax would be planted in an attempt to introduce a new basis for employment in the district.

In July 1848 James Perry and Edward Barrington of the Central Relief

Committee visited the project to prepare a report on the operations and they found that the enterprise was not proceeding as well as had been hoped. The turnip crop had suffered badly from "fly" and had to be resown, some of it three or even four times, the peas and beans were generally poor and had been badly cultivated, while the parsnips, carrots, mangolds and flax were suffering from being sown late and were not well advanced. Wheat, barley and oats had been sown using dibbling and had failed without exception, from which they concluded that dibbling was not suited to the land or climate. The labour costs were found to be excessive and, in summary, it was concluded that the local committee was to blame for the shortcomings and that a first rate man should be sent without delay to take it over. In mitigation of these findings, the report conceded that a great deal of relief had been offered to the destitute that would not otherwise been available.

In August 1848 Arthur Barrington was appointed to go to Ballina to take over the superintendence of the spade cultivation scheme, for which he was to be paid £5 a week plus a travelling allowance. In the following November James Ganly, a Dublin auctioneer, visited Ballina to see about selling the produce of the farm. He advertised the crops for sale but got no offers and instead he recommended selling them by retail to the poor people of the neighbourhood. James Ganly kindly waived his professional fee for his services, accepting only his expenses. Arthur Barrington was also generous to the committee, writing to say that the £5 per week salary and £1 per day travelling expenses due to him was, he considered, too much in the circumstances. He felt that the results of the undertaking had not been satisfactory, and that his five month stay had been much longer than originally intended. While he did not blame himself for either of these circumstances he felt that he should only be given the salary for half the time, regretting that he could not reduce it further due to the heavy expenses he had incurred.

In March 1849 Messrs. Bernard and Kock of Newport, Co. Mayo, offered to buy the flax from the Ballina project at £3 a ton and this was agreed. It was also agreed to advance them a loan of £500 to assist in the setting up of a factory for steeping and preparing flax, while Colonel Knox Gore, a local landowner, was to be advanced £400 for the erection of a flax scutching mill nearby. In October 1850 a claim was received from Hay

Brothers & Co., who were associated with Bernard and Kock, as it had been found that a large portion of the flax purchased in 1849 was unsound. After brief correspondence it was agreed that a full refund at £3 per ton for 40 tons would be allowed.

Auxiliary Relief Committee, Society of Friends,

Limerick, 4th Mo., 1848.

This Committee believing that much good would result by the encouragement of the culture and manufacture of Flax amongst the destitute poor, for their own use as well as for sale, thus affording employment to many women and children, and encouraging habits of industry and cleanliness amongst them, have concluded to make grants of Flax-seed, on Loan, to approved applicants for the use of the poor in their respective neighbourhoods, such applicant to be accountable to this committee for three-fourths the amount of the grant, and to be refunded either in cash or well prepared flax, the remaining one-fourth to be allowed as a bonus to the grower for punctual payment when the crop is ready for market, and at least one-half of the produce must be spun and made up for the use of each family.

*Decision of the Limerick Auxiliary Committee to encourage the growing of flax*

At the end of the project a total of nearly £7,500 had been spent, while the return from crops sold had come to only about £1,750, leaving a shortfall of around £5,700. It had never been intended that this undertaking should pay its way and while the income from the sale of the crops was far below that which was expected, it was felt that the outlay had provided a large amount of employment for the destitute while also teaching them how to cultivate crops that were not normally grown in this part of Ireland, but which would probably become more common through the demise of the potato.

Perhaps the greatest beneficiaries of this project were the owners of the land, as it had become weed-infested and of poor quality through under-use and the intensive cultivation and manuring carried out during the spade cultivation experiment would have returned it to a more favourable state.

## Other agricultural projects

In 1847, Lord Wallscourt of Ardfry, Co. Galway, had been given a loan from the committee for a similar project to that at Ballina on 50 acres of his land. He was advanced £200 on his own security and successfully cultivated the land, giving employment to numerous destitute people. In the spring of 1848 he applied to the committee for permission to retain the £200 in order to put it to similar use for a second season. This was agreed, and Lord Wallscourt was encouraged to double the amount of land with the promise of double the loan. While he did not take up the additional offer, he went ahead with his original scheme, planting 25 acres of turnips, 10 of cabbages, 3 of carrots, 2 of parsnips and 10 of barley dibbled in rather than ploughed and seeded. At the end of the season Lord Wallscourt repaid the loan and the committee was happy with the outcome.

Early in 1849 Colonel Knox Gore of Belleek Manor, Co. Mayo, sought a loan of £800 to enable him to reclaim 100 acres of waste land into cultivation. He was one of the landowners who had granted the use of land for the Ballina experiment and he was sufficiently impressed by the degree to which the local people were assisted by this scheme that he decided to undertake a similar scheme himself. He had arranged to cultivate 200 acres at his own expense and the loan from the committee allowed him to increase this to 300. During the course of the work he carried out a great deal of improvement to the land, which had previously been occupied by tenants who had emigrated to America in 1846. Some 9,000 metres of useless ditches and banks were levelled and land was drained and subsoiled, the cost of these improvements being provided through loans from the Board of Works under the Land Improvement Act.

Colonel Knox Gore sowed 100 acres with oats and barley, 100 acres of flax and 100 acres of turnips. The flax was sown as a result of the decision of Messrs Bernard and Kock to set up a flax steeping plant at Ballina, following which Colonel Knox Gore had spent £1,000 on the construction of a flax scutching mill, with a loan from the Central Relief Committee, as has already been noted. As with so many of the employment creation schemes set up at this time the ultimate financial success of Colonel Knox Gore's exercise was hampered by the poor state of the market for the produce. He found it difficult to sell the turnips and used them as animal fodder, though the sale of his cattle was affected by the cost of bringing them to Liverpool where they were sold. However, he was very optimistic and believed that the following year's crop would benefit so much from the intensive cultivation of the land that the added price would make up the loss incurred through his spade cultivation scheme. His optimism was not misplaced and his increased yield justified the whole project in financial terms.

From the point of view of the Central Relief Committee, the success of the project could be measured in the employment provided. Colonel Knox Gore's report to the committee in August 1850 noted that the Ballina poor law union had been in a most hopeless state due to the large number of destitute people who were being fed on a daily basis. In September 1849 the union was in such a precarious state that it sought, and got, a loan of £100 from the Central Relief Committee to help it out of financial difficulties. The spade cultivation projects improved matters to the extent that they saved the Ballina union some £25,000 a year.

During the famine the Rev. Sidney Smith of Brookeboro, Co. Fermanagh had successfully brought relief to the poor by distributing corn and green crop seeds provided by the Central Relief Committee and in March 1849 he sought a loan from the committee to take this a stage further by cultivating 50 acres using spade labour. It was agreed that £350 would be advanced to him. Some £250 of this sum was expended in wages to labourers and the remaining £100 in seeds and this employed some 120 labourers for several months. Unfortunately, the yield of the crops was below expectations. Just as at Ballina, the turnips were attacked by fly and those that were successfully grown were found to be difficult to sell. In the following year the wheat and oats that were planted were attacked by worm. By March 1852 only £50 of this loan had been repaid and following careful consideration the committee agreed that in the circumstances they would only seek the repayment of £125 of the outstanding amount.

In August 1849 Henry Christy of the London committee passed on to the Central Relief Committee a proposal by Sir John Young of Co. Cavan for the spade labour of 40 to 50 Irish acres, for which he sought a loan of £300. This was granted to him.

## Assessment

There were two main objects behind the Central Relief Committee's advancement of loans for the cultivation of land. Firstly, it was considered that the provision of relief through useful labour was a more satisfactory way of granting aid than through gratuitous distribution of food or money. This system helped to keep the self respect of the recipients, a fact which became clear when labourers were employed who had previously been in receipt of gratuitous relief and who had lost some of their ability to work under a disciplined regime. Secondly, the agricultural projects were designed to show the labourers new methods and new crops as a means of overcoming the problem of over reliance on the now unreliable potato. In these two respects the programmes were undeniably successful. Large numbers of people were provided with incomes so that they and their families no longer had to depend on the poor law unions for outdoor relief. Stories came back to the committee of labourers who when applying for jobs explained that they "had worked with the Quakers last year".

There is no doubt that many of the agricultural experiments were financially disappointing and would tend to dissuade potential future proposers from similar exercises. The experiences of Colonel Knox Gore showed, however, that persistence and good management could lead to success in the medium term.

In addition to these factors there were also spin-off effects of these projects. A major one was that idle land had been thoroughly worked over so that it would be in better condition for future cultivation. There was also the effect on the provision of outdoor relief as was mentioned by some of the commentators such as Rev. Sidney Smith and Colonel Knox Gore. When large numbers of people were given work there was a consequent reduction in the numbers requiring to be fed at the expense of the poor law union. The savings were reflected in the rates struck by the union, and Rev. Sidney Smith claimed that while the rate struck in Fermanagh was as high as five to seven shillings, in the poor law district from which his labourers were drawn it was a mere ten pence, or just 16% to 12% of the rate struck in other districts.

# CHAPTER FOURTEEN:
# ASSISTANCE TO INDUSTRY

It was generally recognised in the 1840's that the population of Ireland was too dependent on agriculture and that the industry of the country was under-developed. Large numbers of people were living on land holdings that were too small for more than subsistence, a point which was a principal factor which led to the failure of a single crop becoming a major disaster. For three decades before the famine Irish agriculture had been moving away from tillage into cattle with severe consequences for the numbers of jobs for labourers on farms. In 1845, the same year as the potato blight appeared in Ireland Dr (later Sir) Robert Kane published his book *The Industrial Resources of Ireland* in which he argued that Ireland had a huge potential for industrial development and that Irish made products could compete on a solid economic footing with English manufactures.

As a result of these factors, the provision of industrial employment during the famine had the joint advantages of providing jobs for the immediate relief of the destitute, and helping towards the longer term restructuring of the Irish economy. These issues were not lost on the Quaker relief committees and opportunities to foster new industry were rarely missed. In some of these cases the industries were closely related to other branches of employment which was being assisted, such as the curing plants associated with the fisheries.

As early as January 1847, when the committee's relief system was only getting going, a request came in from a John Hamilton in Donegal seeking help with his proposal to set up a small manufacturing business among the peasantry. The committee responded with a grant of £100.

In the spring of that year another Donegal resident, Francis Forster of Dungloe, proposed to set up plant for the production of kelp for which he was advanced a loan of £200. A year later, in April 1848, he wrote in strong terms to the committee describing the hardships he would be exposed to if he was to be held to the repayment of the loan. Some 189 tons of kelp had been purchased with a value of £358, but ultimately the project was not profitable. The committee decided to relinquish its claim against him in exchange for the £15 or so which remained in his care.

The committee's attention had often been drawn to the potential for flannel manufacture in Ireland, where there was ample supply of wool and there were streams suitable for water power. In an attempt to establish such an industry enquiries were made with a view to finding a suitable person for the task. James Hack Tuke, the Quaker from York who had toured the country in the previous year, wrote to the committee in February 1848 suggesting the name of James Townsend of Yorkshire whom he believed to be suitable. James Townsend attended a meeting of the Central Relief Committee at the beginning of March 1848, following which he was given a letter of introduction to Thomas Clibborn of Moate who had offered to assist. Together, the two men then toured Mayo and west Galway seeking a suitable spot for the proposed flannel industry, concluding that Erris did not have sufficient supplies of wool. In Connemara there appeared to be a considerable supply of wool of good quality and they also found some machinery for preparing and spinning wool which the owner offered to sell for £100. James Townsend estimated that his enterprise would require £500 for the purchase of machinery and working capital of £1,000 to £2,000, for which he would employ between 130 and 150 people. The committee concluded that it could not undertake to supply this amount of capital alone, though it would be prepared to advance up to £1,500 as a loan secured on the machinery and stock if one or two suitable persons with the skill and knowledge required could be found to take on the project. The offer was not taken up and the opportunity was lost.

The Belfast Ladies Industrial Association for Connaught sought a grant in May 1848 towards its work in establishing industrial schools throughout the west where young women and girls would be taught needlework on the model of similar schools set up in Ulster. The committee decided that it would advance a grant of £500 provided the association was able to match this sum from other sources. This took more than six months, but they were finally able to announce to the committee on 28th December that they had collected £502 18s 9d and the committee released its grant of £500.

As we have already seen, a spin-off from the spade cultivation project at Ballina was that the firm of Bernard and Kock, which had purchased the flax crop, decided to establish a plant for steeping and preparing flax according to the most modern principles and this was to be run by the local firm of Hay Brothers. The committee advanced a loan of £500 for this purpose. At the same time Colonel Knox Gore proposed to build a flax scutching mill near Ballina and it was agreed to advance him £400 towards the costs. The mill cost the Colonel £1,000 but he only took up £200 of the loan offered and he repaid this in March 1851. Arthur Barrington, who inspected the enterprise in July 1849 when Bernard and Kock's mill was under construction, reported that Colonel Gore had about eighty acres of flax sown, another landowner had forty acres, while there were numerous patches on other farms of three acres and more, so that there would be a good supply of flax for the mill. Two years later the amount of flax grown locally had grown to 350 acres, though the yield, at $2\frac{1}{2}$ tons per acre, was low in many instances through inadequate cultivation. In other cases yields reached $3\frac{1}{2}$ tons and this would supply a good return to the farmer.

At the flax mill Hay Brothers employed a constant labour force of a hundred.

The Ladies Industrial Society of Grafton Street, Dublin approached the committee in March 1852 seeking a grant towards the support of a school for instructing young women in the making of lace which had been established under their care at Wentworth Place, Dublin. A grant of £100 was agreed.

# CHAPTER FIFTEEN:

# COLMANSTOWN MODEL FARM

By the summer of 1848 the spade cultivation project at Ballina was nearing its conclusion as the crops approached their harvest. At the same time, the distribution of relief through soup kitchens and other food supplies was coming to an end following the introduction of the government's new relief measures. It was just at this time that an approach was made to the Central Relief Committee by Dr Bewley, a Quaker from Moate, Co Westmeath, who suggested that a model farm should be established and as a result it was decided to lease a suitable farm for the purpose.

Dr Bewley proposed that a farm be established to act as a model which could demonstrate how farms could be organised efficiently and profitably. There would also be an agricultural school where methods of farming could be taught so as to improve the knowledge of the small farmer and labourer in the use of various farm implements and the growing of alternative crops and keeping of livestock.

Despite the desperate state of agriculture in Ireland at this time it did not prove to be easy to find a suitable farm and the committee was on the point of giving up when, in February 1849, a farm of 650 statute acres was found in east Galway at Colmanstown. The land was of reasonable quality, but needed a great deal of work to bring it up to the standard required for the project. A lease was taken for 999 years, with three members of the committee being appointed as trustees, and the project got under way.

The Central Relief Committee drew up a management plan which set down the aims of the project. The farm was to be run without subsidy once the initial costs of setting it up were met and was to avoid experimental methods so as to avoid risking losses. The day to day running would be in the hands of a farm manager, who would report to a management committee of five Quakers and this committee, in turn, would be appointed by a board of directors consisting of thirty Quakers appointed by an annual general meeting which would be open to all members of the Society of Friends.

The farm was set up with £12,000 of capital which was used to reclaim land, drain and subsoil it, lay out roads and watercourses and provide buildings. A short time after the farm was established some 228 workers were employed on the land and after a time a fine range of farm buildings had been erected, including a water wheel to run a threshing machine and a corn mill. Once it was in operation the farm included a wide range of livestock such as cattle, pigs and sheep, together with meadows and oats, barley, turnip and other crops.

*Surviving buildings at Colmanstown Model Farm, Co. Galway*

The model farm at Colmanstown continued in operation long after the Central Relief Committee's other famine works had ceased and only came to an end in 1863 during another food crisis when the decision was taken to close the farm and dispose of the lease. The work carried out continued to be of benefit as the farm was run for another century as a single unit, only being subdivided in the 1960's. Many of the farm roads and some of the farm buildings remain to show the scale of this imaginative project.

# CHAPTER SIXTEEN:

# CONCLUSION OF RELIEF WORKS

With the exception of the model farm at Colmanstown and the short burst of relief operations in July and August, the Quaker relief committees wound down their operations from the early part of 1849. The work of the Central Relief Committee came to concentrate on the continued monitoring of projects already under way such as the fisheries at Castletown and a few minor grants of aid. At the same time the question of the publication of the final report came to prominence. Between these two items of business the committee was very much less busy than it had been. From November 1846 to April 1849 the Central Relief Committee had met more or less every Thursday, with additional meetings whenever necessary, including, on one occasion, meetings three days in a row. The number dropped to one meeting a month in May and June 1849, returned to weekly meetings for the seven week relief operations in July and August after which it reduced again. From 1850 to 1852 the committee met infrequently, sometimes several months would elapse with no meeting and they were generally called only when there was business to transact, such as the receipt of reports and the making of decisions relating to the final report.

A large amount of the workload of the committee had been related to the amount of direct relief being offered through grants of food, clothing and money. As this reduced there was a corresponding reduction in the workload for the staff employed and in April 1849 it was decided to close down the office in Fleet Street. Pim Brothers and Company, the family firm of Jonathan Pim, kindly offered the use of a room in its house at 22 William Street South free of rent and the decision was taken to move there. Notice was given to the various employees and to the committee for winding up the Agricultural and Commercial Bank and the assistant secretary, Samuel Darton, was instructed to move to the new premises.

# CHAPTER SEVENTEEN:

# PREPARING THE *TRANSACTIONS*

As the operations were winding down, the committee was able to turn its attention to preparing a report to the public. This matter arose at a committee meeting in February 1851 and while the concept was considered important the two Honorary Secretaries made it clear that they would not be able to produce the document. The committee accepted this and resolved to seek "some literary man of approved talent" to take on the task.

The basis for the report was set down in memoranda by Joseph Bewley, the Honorary Secretary who had been the instigator of the relief operations. Arrangements were made with Professor Hancock of Trinity College, Dublin for the preparation of the final report, but before he could start he was forced to stand down as a result of an increase in his college workload. Shortly after this Joseph Bewley died and given the reduced level of operations it was not considered necessary to replace him so that Jonathan Pim continued as the sole Honorary Secretary. On the recommendation of Professor Hancock an approach was made to Professor William E. Hearn of Queen's College, Galway, who agreed to undertake the task of preparing the report. By late November 1851 the first draft was ready for the committee but it was to be several months more before it began to take shape. In March 1852 the text was put in type and it was decided to give a copy to each member of the committee. At this stage Jonathan Pim stated his concern at the sections in the text which dealt with land law. While he was something of an expert on the subject and had written a book expounding his views, he felt that the Central Relief Committee was synonymous in the public mind with the Society of Friends and it would be unsuitable for any publication which appeared to come from that Society to contain a treatise on political economy. Having said this, he admitted that the report would be devalued by the omission of the views of the committee "expressed in as clear and forcible language as we can find" and accepted with reluctance that the subject should remain in the text.

From March to May 1852 the content of the report was debated and discussions were held with the auxiliary committees to ascertain their views. It was agreed that it should be published and a subcommittee was appointed to look after the revision of the draft and to decide whether to include all or part of the appendix. This subcommittee was to consist of Edward Barrington, Edward Alexander, Thomas H. Todhunter, Thomas Bewley, James Perry, Richard Allen and Dr. Joshua Harvey.

By August the report was with the printers and the committee decided to order 1,500 copies of the complete work bound in cloth, while another 1,500 would be printed and bound in paper containing the main report and the accounts but without the rest of the appendices. Of these, 500 of each version would be sent to Friends in New York for distribution to subscribers and, ever mindful of economy, the committee resolved that these copies would be sent unbound as they would be more likely to avoid import duty. A further 500 copies were to be distributed amongst those in England and Ireland who had contributed to the funds and copies were to be sold through bookshops in Dublin and London. The published volume was entitled *Transactions of the Central Relief Committee of the Society of Friends during the Famine in Ireland in 1846 and 1847* and contains 130 pages of report and 340 pages of appendices and has become the main source of information on Quaker relief work during the famine.

# CHAPTER EIGHTEEN:
# LOBBYING AND OTHER CAMPAIGNS

The work carried out by the Quaker committees covered a wide range of operations. In many of these, as we have seen, Quakers campaigned for changes in the law, or in the relief system which was being operated by the government. Aspects such as the distribution of government relief, the use of relief works and the charting of the ocean for fishing purposes were actively pursued by the London and Dublin committees. In addition, there were other aspects which had no direct bearing to the relief operations but which reflected aspects of Quaker ethos.

In the autumn of 1846 a suggestion was made that the use of barley in distilleries was immoral when so many people faced starvation. This viewpoint was influenced by the Quaker stance on alcohol which encouraged members of the Society of Friends to avoid the use of distilled spirits except for medicinal purposes. In the previous decade the Quaker views on alcohol had led William Martin, a Cork Friend, to encourage Father Mathew to take up the cause of temperance in Ireland. Early in 1847 the London committee lobbied the government in relation to the distillers use of barley, and five members of the committee met the prime minister, Lord John Russell, but failed to get a ban imposed. The Quaker disapproval of alcohol was mainly aimed at spirits at this time, while the use of beer was only frowned upon if taken to excess. Hence the Central Relief Committee saw no contradiction in seeking a ban on the manufacture of spirits while accepting donations from a brewery. The amount of funds collected in Ireland from non-Quakers was relatively small, at £374, and more than half of this came from Arthur Guinness, Son and Company, in two donations of £100 each.

Another issue which was taken up related to a Royal proclamation which declared that 27th March 1847 would be a public day of fast and humiliation to offer prayers for the end of the famine. Quakers at this time observed no holy feast days, including Christmas and Easter, believing that outward observance of prayer was unnatural and that each day should be equally marked with humility and spiritual observance. It was also felt that the use of such proclamations by civil government to impose such specific acts of worship was contrary to their views of the spirituality of true worship and was an infringement of the rights of conscience. These points were published in the Quaker journal *The Friend* as a reminder to Quakers, but the editor was very careful not to make any suggestion that the proclamation should be disobeyed - such a choice would be up to the individual.

*Lime kiln at Colmanstown Model Farm*

# CHAPTER NINETEEN:

# AFTERMATH

By the time the *Transactions* had been published the work of the committees had come to an end. The model farm at Colmanstown continued to operate, overseen by its directors and management committee and it did not need any additional input from the Central Relief Committee. That committee did not lay itself down, though, perhaps not seeing that any formal decision was necessary. Its meetings had, after all, become less and less frequent over the previous three years as its work had diminished.

For almost ten years after August 1852 the Central Relief Committee in Dublin lay dormant. Then, following a particularly bad harvest in the autumn of 1861, hunger returned to Ireland. In January 1862 matters had become sufficiently critical that the committee was reconvened to consider recommencing relief operations. To replace committee members who had died seven new members were appointed - John Webb junior, Thomas W. Fisher, John Barrington, Henry Wigham, Charles G. Malone, Thomas Pim junior and Robert G. Gatchell. As before, a subcommittee was established to handle applications for relief and from the middle of February grants were made.

The committee also renewed its contacts with the secretary of the London committee. The Central Relief Committee's own funds which remained amounted to £3,583, including interest of £954 received since 1851. Over the next while the committee dispensed grants of money in the way that it had in 1847. It was following this that the decision was made that the model farm at Colmanstown had outlived its usefulness and that it should be sold. It is possible that the farm had suffered bad harvests in 1861 and that its financial position was weak.

When the Central Relief Committee finally decided that its task was completed and that it should be wound up, there remained the decision as to the disposal of the remaining funds. It was decided that all money in hand should be given over to a suitable charity and the choice was a hospital. In 1811 the Society of Friends had established a hospital in Donnybrook, near Dublin to treat Quakers suffering from disorders of the mind though it was not to this establishment that the surplus funds would be given, but to the hospital next door, then known as the Royal Hospital for Incurables. It is more than likely that the choice resulted from a sense of fair play, in that the funds had originated from a wide variety of sources in Ireland, England and America and were intended for the help of the population of Ireland in general and not for the Society of Friends. The donation of the surplus to an institution which served only one section of the community would have been contrary to the spirit in which funds had been subscribed.

## The famine and Quakers

The effects of the famine were greatest on the families of the landless labourers and the small farmers, but gradually the entire economic system was affected and assistance came to be needed by a great variety of people in all manner of occupations. Quakers did not escape from this although the Society of Friends would have had a high proportion of town-dwellers, merchants and millers amongst its members rather than small farmers. It is likely that many Quaker businesses suffered severely in the famine, one such example being that of Joseph Beale of Mountmellick, a manufacturer of woollens and cotton who also had a corn mill. The economic slump caused by the famine ruined his textile business while the corn mill could operate only sporadically as grain was available. By the end of the famine he was financially ruined and he and his family emigrated to Australia. Also in Mountmellick there was a Quaker school which provided education for the children of Quakers living in Leinster. This school was almost forced to close due to the effects of the famine on its own potato crop which resulted in a large increase in expenditure in an attempt to purchase food on the open market.

The precise extent of the losses caused to Quaker businesses and Quaker families during the famine is unknown as is the exact degree of achievement and loss experienced by Quaker relief workers. A fundamental aspect of Quakerism is humility so that achievements would not be broadcast and, in particular, individuals would not be singled out for praise. This practice was illustrated by obituaries in Quaker publications which tended to concentrate on the spiritual aspects of the deceased rather than material achievements or charitable works. Another example was the disapproval of any kind of monument to individuals so that the use of grave stones was not the norm in Quaker burial grounds until the 1850's, while until the late 19th century few Quakers had their portraits painted. It can be difficult, therefore, to piece together details of the involvement of individual Quakers or the degree of stress or ill health which they experienced. If this ethos of humility had not existed the *Transactions* would probably have included an appendix listing the names of those who died in the course of providing relief to the suffering, possibly with brief accounts of what they had achieved and how they came to die.

We know from correspondence that Jonathan Pim almost suffered a severe health breakdown in the spring of 1847 as a direct result of the weight of work he was carrying as one of the Honorary Secretaries of the Central Relief Committee. The other Hon. Secretary, Joseph Bewley, did not survive, collapsing and dying while on a walk with his family in 1851 at the age of 56, apparently as a result of a heart attack arising from the strain of almost five years' involvement with the Central Relief Committee. Jacob Harvey, the New York Friend who was the Central Relief Committee's main contact in the United States, died in 1848 during the height of the famine as a result of over-exertion while trying to assist the huge influx of Irish immigrants. William Todhunter, a member of the Central Relief Committee, died in 1850 at the age of 46 after his health broke down from his exertions in famine relief. He had been heavily involved in the attempts to improve the fisheries and had spent some months on the trawler the *Erne* off the west coast.

Information is particularly lacking in relation to the number of Quakers who may have died of fever contracted while assisting the famine victims. The survival rate amongst relief workers who contracted fever was poor as they would have had less immunity to certain of the fevers than those they were helping who were more frequently exposed to the disease. Many relief workers of all creeds and backgrounds died and Quakers were no exception, perhaps the best known victim being Abraham Beale of the Cork auxiliary committee who died of typhus fever in August 1847 at the age of 54. In other cases the deaths of Quakers were announced in the media such as that of Matthew Jenkinson of Carlow who died of typhus fever in March 1847 aged about 58. In the same month William Forster's party was delayed at Manorhamilton, Co. Leitrim, where one of its members, J. C. Harvey, had contracted fever. In June 1847 it was reported that fever was raging in Cork and that several Friends had been attacked with it, one of whom had died.

## Long term influences

None of the Quakers who had been involved in the relief efforts would have remained untouched by the experience. As William Bennett observed during his tour in Mayo:

> My hand trembles while I write. The scenes of human misery and degradation we witnessed still haunt my imagination, with the vividness and power of some horrid and tyrannous delusion, rather than the features of a sober reality.

The Society of Friends as a body had discovered a niche wherein it could offer a concerted programme of aid in a crisis and this experience was used from time to time through the rest of the century, blossoming into a more formal structure of relief in the twentieth century with the establishment of the Friends Service Council.

The effect on children who saw the misery of the famine must have been intense and this would include Joseph Rowntree, a member of the York family of confectioners, who visited Ireland with his father during the famine when he was fourteen years old. Scenes he saw stayed with him and later influenced him in his work to combat poverty, including the establishment of three charitable trusts, the best known of which survives as the Rowntree Trust.

One Quaker couple, James and Mary Ellis, were inspired by the relief operations to take up a radical personal role in combating poverty in Ireland. They came from Leicester where James Ellis was a flour miller and later a worsted manufacturer and in 1849 when he was 56 they left England and purchased an estate of 1,800 acres at Letterfrack, Co. Galway. There they employed some eighty local people to help to reclaim land for agriculture and they built cottages and other buildings to transform Letterfrack into a thriving village. There James Ellis taught agriculture and building while Mary Ellis worked to ease the poverty of the locality. They remained at Letterfrack until 1857 when their health was failing and they sold the property and returned to England. They left behind them a thriving community that to this day has traces of their work such as osiers growing which are descended from those planted to provide material for basket making, and fuschia bushes growing along the roadside on the way from Westport.

*Jonathan Pim, one of the Secretaries of the Central Relief Committee*

The member of the Central Relief Committee who was to become the most prominent was Jonathan Pim. He was a member of a well known Dublin family of textile manufacturers and was forty years of age when the Central Relief Committee was established. As we have seen he came to realise just how much the land system was contributing to the continuing problems in Ireland and published a book on the subject entitled *The Condition and Prospects of Ireland and evils arising from the present distribution of landed property.* This book was widely distributed to influential people, particularly members of parliament, when it was published in 1848 and when a new land bill was introduced he had extensive negotiations with the government to seek modifications. This bill was enacted as the Encumbered Estates Act in 1849 and was the beginnings of the massive changes in whole land system in Ireland in the latter half of the 19th century. Jonathan Pim continued to campaign for reform in land law and was elected to parliament in 1865 as a member for Dublin. It is thought that he may have been the author of the Land Acts of 1870 and 1881 which were crucial points in Gladstone's reform of the Irish land system. He also continued to write, publishing *The Land Question in Ireland* in 1867, *Ireland and the Imperial Parliament* in 1871, and *A Review of the Economic and Social Progress of Ireland since the Famine* in 1876. He died in 1886.

# CHAPTER TWENTY:

# CONCLUSION

During its relief works the Central Relief Committee handled almost £200,000 worth of aid, equivalent to not far short of £11 million at today's prices. The source of these donations was varied, some locally raised but most coming from outside Ireland. In all, about £62,000 was donated as money, £134,000 in food, £147 as soup boilers, £200 in clothing from the Commissary-General and the rest, some £1,800, was raised in interest on funds.

It will never be possible to say how much was the total contribution from Irish Friends, either in terms of the work put in or of the donations, as most of this went unrecorded in the local efforts to tackle the famine. Over and above their local contributions, Irish Friends contributed £4,826 to the Central Relief Committee's work.

The London committee managed to raise a total of almost £43,000, of which the majority, amounting to £37,400, was handed over to the Central Relief Committee in Dublin. Donations amounting to more than £4,000 were received from non-Friends in Ireland and Great Britain and in addition to the money donations substantial quantities of clothing was provided in a concerted effort by communities all over England and the United States.

The donations from the United States were so great as to virtually overshadow all other sources. This was partly a result of the publicity organised by Quakers but was also due to the Quaker organisation providing a suitable channel through which relief could be brought to those who needed it efficiently and effectively.

The £200,000 worth of Quaker relief seems small in comparison with £390,000 handled by the British Relief Association and about £10 million from the government, but it must not be forgotten how small the Society of Friends was in relation to the population as a whole. The efforts put in by this small band of workers left its impression on the Irish mind due to the wide range of relief offered and the even hand with which it was distributed. It is a mark of the ultimate success of the operations that the Quaker relief work is still remembered all over Ireland today.

# APPENDIX ONE:

# MEMBERS OF THE RELIEF COMMITTEES

The following list includes members of the Central Relief Committee, its corresponding members, the auxiliary committees and the London committee. It is not possible to list all the names of the members of each of the subcommittees. For the most part these were made up from those whose names are listed below.

## Central Relief Committee

Alexander, Edward
Allen, Joseph
Allen, Richard
Barrington, Edward
Barrington, Richard
Bewley, Joseph  (Secretary and Treasurer)
Bewley, Samuel
Bewley, Thomas
Doyle, William
Harvey, Joshua, M.D.
Hogg, William
Malone, William
Perry, Henry
Perry, James  (Treasurer)
Pim, James, junior
Pim, Jonathan  (Secretary)
Pim, Thomas
Pim, Thomas, junior  (Treasurer)
Pim, William Harvey
Robinson, William
Russell, Henry
Todhunter, Thomas H.
Todhunter, William
Woods, Adam

## Corresponding members

Abell, John, of Limerick
Barcroft, William J. of Moy
Beale, Abraham, of Cork
Clibborn, Thomas, of Moate
Dowd, Richard, of Roscrea
Forbes, James, of Kildare
Goodbody, Marcus, of Clara
Grubb, Benjamin, of Clonmel
Hancock, Thomas of Lisburn
Harvey, Thomas, of Youghal
Haughton, Joseph, of Ferns
Jacob, Thomas White, of Waterford
Malcomson, Joseph, of Portlaw
Pike, Ebenezer, of Cork
Pike, Jonathan, of Dungannon
Pim, John, junior, of Belfast
Pim, Thomas Thacker, of Mountmellick
Richardson, James N. of Lisburn
Strangman, Joshua W., of Waterford
Wakefield, Thomas C. of Moyallen
Woods, William, of Limerick


## Cork Auxiliary Committee

Beale, Abraham
Beale, Joshua
Fisher, Abraham, of Youghal
Harvey, William
Harvey, Joseph
Harvey, Thomas, of Youghal
Pike, Ebenezer
Wright, Thomas

## Waterford Auxiliary Committee

Allen, Richard
Jacob, Thomas W.
Richardson, Joseph S.
Strangman, Joshua William
Strangman, Thomas H.
Walpole, James
White, George
White, Samuel
White, Thomas Robinson

## Clonmel Auxiliary Committee

Clibborn, Barclay
Clibborn, Joseph
Davis, Robert
Davis, William
Fayle, Samuel
Grubb, Benjamin
Grubb, Joseph
Grubb, Thomas J.
Hughes, John
Hughes, Thomas
Malcomson, Joshua
Pim, John T.

## Limerick Auxiliary Committee

Abell, John
Alexander, James
Alexander, Samuel
Alexander, William
Fitt, Thomas
Harvey, James
Unthank, Isaac W.
Woods, William

**Committee of the Society of Friends in London**

Allcard, John
Barclay, Joseph G.
Christy, Henry
Coventry, Millis
Forster, Josiah
Forster, Robert
Forster, William
Foster, Joseph T.
Fowler, Thomas  (Treasurer)
Fox, Francis
Fox, Samuel
Godlee, Rickman  (Secretary)
Gurney, Samuel
Harris, Edward
Hodgkin, John
Lister, Joseph J.
Norton, Thomas, junior
Stacey, George
Sturge, Samuel
Tylor, Charles  (Secretary)


**Sources:** *Transactions of the Central Relief Committee* Appendix I and Appendix II

# APPENDIX TWO:
# MEMBERS OF THE CHARLES STREET SOUP SHOP SUBCOMMITTEE

The subcommittee appointed by the Central Relief Committee to set up and run the soup kitchen in Charles Street worked in close co-operation with a committee of women Friends. The subcommittee consisted of about ten Friends initially but reconstituted itself in the light of experience and co-opted new members. The large group of workers looked after the running of the soup shop twice a day, six days a week on a rota basis.

The following Friends were involved with the running of the soup shop for at least part of its six-month existence:

| | |
|---|---|
| Allen, Alexander | Garrett, Joseph |
| Allen, Anne | Gatchell, Robert G. (Treasurer) |
| Allen, Charlotte | Goff, Sarah |
| Allen, Ellen | Green, John |
| Allen, Jane | Harvey, Dr |
| Allen, Joseph | Jackson, Alfred |
| Allen, Richard | Kitchin, Phebe |
| Barrington, Elizabeth R | Lamb, Elizabeth |
| Barrington, Margaret | Moss, Mary |
| Barrington, William L | Perry, Henry |
| Beale, Joseph | Pike, Amelia |
| Bewley, Margaret | Pike, Sophia |
| Bewley, Maria | Roberts, Samuel |
| Bewley, Samuel | Robinson, William |
| Bewley, Samuel junior, | Russell, Elizabeth |
| Boardman, Elizabeth | Tollerton, Elizabeth |
| Doyle, Susan | Walpole, Sarah |
| Edmundson, John | Webb, John junior |
| Eves, Charlotte | Woods, Adam (Secretary) |
| Eves, Jane | Woods, Lydia |
| Eves, Joshua | Wright, Jonathan |
| Fennell, Mary | Wright, John |
| Fisher, Thomas | Wright, John junior |

**Source:** Minute book of the soup subcommittee of the Central Relief Committee, held in the National Archives, Dublin.

# APPENDIX THREE:
# RELIEF GRANTED TO EACH COUNTY

The following table shows a breakdown of the amount of certain types of relief which was granted to each county.

## ULSTER

| County | Food (tons) | Boilers | Money (£) | Seeds (lbs.) | Clothing (grants) |
|---|---|---|---|---|---|
| Antrim | 40 | 0 | 300 | | 8 |
| Armagh | 53 | 2 | 248 | 516 | 37 |
| Cavan | 123 | 5 | 172 | 1,096 | 46 |
| Donegal | 400 | 19 | 1,429 | 10,149 | 55 |
| Down | 35 | 1 | 144 | | 16 |
| Fermanagh | 114 | 4 | 316 | 7,409 | 49 |
| Londonderry | 135 | 0 | 197 | | 16 |
| Monaghan | 74 | 1 | 243 | 675 | 32 |
| Tyrone | 104 | 3 | 382 | 380 | 37 |
| **Totals:** | **1,078** | **35** | **3,431** | **20,225** | **296** |

## LEINSTER

| County | Food (tons) | Boilers | Money (£) | Seeds (lbs.) | Clothing (grants) |
|---|---|---|---|---|---|
| Carlow | 34 | 5 | 85 | 62 | 38 |
| Dublin | 61 | 1 | 612 | 280 | 8 |
| Kildare | 15 | 1 | 45 | 526 | 35 |
| Kilkenny | 35 | 12 | 197 | 446 | 17 |
| King's County | 87 | 2 | 175 | 4,380 | 73 |
| Longford | 24 | 1 | 148 | 685 | 24 |
| Louth | 22 | 0 | 5 | | 2 |
| Meath | 13 | 1 | 15 | | 12 |
| Queen's County | 45 | 4 | 165 | 220 | 54 |
| Westmeath | 46 | 0 | 96 | 1,883 | 22 |
| Wexford | 50 | 10 | 240 | 676 | 45 |
| Wicklow | 27 | 0 | 106 | | 23 |
| **Totals:** | **459** | **37** | **1,889** | **9,158** | **353** |

## CONNAUGHT

| County | Food (tons) | Boilers | Money (£) | Seeds (lbs.) | Clothing (grants) |
|---|---|---|---|---|---|
| Galway | 901 | 18 | 1,140 | 24,074 | 107 |
| Leitrim | 126 | 3 | 425 | 8,527 | 49 |
| Mayo | 696 | 29 | 2,309 | 54,172 | 61 |
| Roscommon | 429 | 14 | 708 | 11,595 | 88 |
| Sligo | 230 | 1 | 702 | 7,806 | 53 |
| **Totals:** | **2,382** | **65** | **5,284** | **106,174** | **358** |

## MUNSTER

| County | Food (tons) | Boilers | Money (£) | Seeds (lbs.) | Clothing (grants) |
|---|---|---|---|---|---|
| Clare | 632 | 6 | 993 | 1,933 | 26 |
| Cork | 2,668 | 63 | 4,490 | 24,827 | 112 |
| Kerry | 702 | 9 | 937 | 2,250 | 13 |
| Limerick | 560 | 11 | 1,185 | 1,671 | 20 |
| Tipperary | 550 | 35 | 2,008 | 3,243 | 87 |
| Waterford | 245 | 33 | 474 | | 17 |
| **Totals:** | **5,357** | **157** | **10,087** | **33,924** | **275** |

## TOTALS: IRELAND

| | Food (tons) | Boilers | Money (£) | Seeds (ibs.) | Clothing (grants) |
|---|---|---|---|---|---|
| **Totals:** | **7,848** | **294** | **20,700** | **168,482** | **1,280** |

**Source:** Compiled from information in the *Transactions of the Central Relief Committee*, Appendices XXVIII, XVI and XV. In some cases figures have been amalgamated from more than one source and in all cases they refer to the grants processed through the Central Relief Committee and the auxiliary committees.

# BIBLIOGRAPHY

The following sources have been used in the writing of this book or contain other information which may be helpful to the reader who wishes to pursue specific aspects in more detail:

Beale, Edgar **The Earth Between Them - Joseph Beale's Letters Home to Ireland from Victoria 1852-53** (Sydney, 1975)

Bennett, William **Narrative of a recent journey of Six Weeks in Ireland in connexion with the subject of supplying small seed to some of the remoter districts with current observations on the depressed circumstances of the people, and the means presented for the permanent improvement of their social condition** [this title is normally abbreviated to *Six Weeks in Ireland*] (London and Dublin, 1847)

*The British Friend,* volumes IV (1846) to VII (1849): various articles during the period of the famine.

Burritt, Elihu **A Visit of Three Days to Skibbereen and its Neighbourhood** (London, 1847)

Central Relief Committee of the Society of Friends, minute books and other papers held in the National Archives, Dublin.

Central Relief Committee **Address to the Public from the Relief Association of the Society of Friends in Ireland** (Dublin, 1849)

Central Relief Committee of the Society of Friends *Transactions of the Central Relief Committee of the Society of Friends dnuring the Famine in Ireland 1846 and 1847* (Dublin, 1852)

Clonmel auxiliary committee minute book for 1846-47 in the Grubb Collection, Friends Historical Library, Swanbrook House, Donnybrook, Dublin

Daly, Mary E. **The Famine in Ireland** (Dublin, 1989)

*The Friend,* volumes IV (1846) to VII (1849) various articles during the period of the famine.

Harrison, Richard S. **Cork City Quakers 1655-1939: A Brief History** (Cork, 1991)

Harrison, Richard S. **Richard Davis Webb: Dublin Quaker Printer (1805-72)** (Cork, 1993)

Hatton, Helen E. **The Largest Amount of Good: Quaker Relief in Ireland 1654-1921** (McGill-Queen's University Press, 1993)

Hodgkin Correspondence in the Friends Historical Library, Swanbrook House.

Limerick auxiliary committee minute books for 1847 held in the Friends Historical Library, Swanbrook House.

London committee **Address from the Committee of the Society of Friends in London on the subject of the distress in Ireland** (London, 1846)

Ó Gráda, Cormac **The Great Irish Famine** (Dublin, 1989)

Ó Gráda, Cormac **Ireland before and after the Famine** (Dublin 1988 and 1993)

O'Neill, Thomas P. *The Society of Friends and the Great Famine* **Studies** (June l950)

Pim, Jonathan The **Conditions and Prospects of Ireland and events arising from the present distribution of Landed Property - Suggestions for a Remedy** (Dublin, 1848)

Tuke, James H A **Visit to Connaught in the Autumn of 1847** (London, 1847)

Tully Cross Guild **Portrait of a Parish: Ballynakill, Connemara** [in relation to James and Mary Ellis in Letterfrack] Irish Countrywomen's Association, 1985

Vernon, Anne **Joseph Rowntree**: **A Quaker Businessman**

Wigham, Maurice J **The Irish Quakers** Historical Committee of the Religious Society of Friends in Ireland (1992)

Yearly Meeting of Friends in Ireland **Rules of Discipline of the Yearly Meeting of Friends in Ireland** (Dublin, 1841)

# INDEX

Board of Works, loans, 62
Boardman, Elizabeth, 87
Boyle, 46
Brett, Henry, 59
brewery, 74
Bridge Street, Upper, 41, 44
British Relief Association,
    43, 47, 82
Brookeboro, county Fermanagh, 63
Burgoyne, Sir John, 35
Bushe, Charles, 51

Campbell, William T., 51
Carlow, county, amount of relief, 88
Carribean Islands, 24
Castletown, Berehaven,
    51, 52, 53, 55, 56, 71
Cavan, county, 17, 64
    amount of relief, 88
Central Relief Committee:
    address to Irish Quakers, 8
    address to public, 1848, 26
    composition, 4
    corresponding members,
        5, 25, 33, 84
    dormancy, 76
    ethics, 24
    finances, 82
    formation of, 4
    funds, 76
    interim report, 26
    investments, 15
    meetings of, 71
    members, 83
    office, 13, 14, 16
    organisation, 12
    premises, 14, 15, 16, 41, 44
    reconvened 1862, 76
    staff, 13, 15, 16, 71
    subcommittees, 12, 13, 15
    winding up, 76

Chard, Captain Arthur, 54
Charles Street, soup kitchen, 28, 29, 37, 87
Charleston, 24
charts, coastal, 53, 54, 56, 74
Christmas, 74
Christy, Henry, 64, 86
Claddagh, the, 48, 49, 54
Clare, county, 18
Clare, county, amount of relief, 89
Clibborn:
    Barclay, 85
    Joseph, 85
    Thomas, 67, 84
Clifden, 34, 51
Clonmel, 25
    auxiliary committee, 6, 20, 37
        members, 85
    soup kitchen, 28
clothing, 40
    donations, 23, 82
    subcommittee, 40
    amounts distributed, 88
Cloyne, 55
Coalbrookdale Iron Company, 30
coastguard, 49
Cochrane, Henry, 44
Cole Alley, Dublin, 44
Colmanstown, 69, 71, 76
commissariat, government, 35
Commissary General, 82
Connaught, 15, 18, 35
    amount of relief, 89
Connemara, 67
Cork 22, 25, 33, 51, 74
    auxiliary committee
        6, 20, 34, 36, 37, 46, 55, 78
        members, 84
    clothing subcommittee, 45
    fever in, 79
    Monthly Meeting, 6
    soup kitchen, 29

Cork, county, 18
    amount of relief, 89
    clothing grants, 43, 44
    seed distribution, 47
correspondence, American, 26
correspondence, extracts from, 25
corresponding members, 5, 25, 33, 84
Coventry, Millis, 86
crime, 19
Crosfield, Joseph, 17

Darby, Abraham and Alfred, 30
Darton, Samuel, 71
Davis, Robert, 20, 85
Davis, William, 85
Derrynane Abbey, 55
distilleries, 74
Dominican Order, 54
donations, 21, 22
Donegal, county, 17, 66
    amount of relief, 88
    clothing grants, 44
    seed distribution, 46
Dorcas Institute, 40
Dowd, Richard, 84
Down, county, amount of relief, 88
Doyle, Susan, 87
Doyle, William, 40, 83
Drummond, W & Sons,
    seed merchants, 46
Dublin, county, amount of relief, 88
Dublin, soup kitchen, 28, 29
Dunfanaghy, 34
Dungarvan, 48
Dungloe, 66
Dunmore East, 55

Easter, 74
Eastwood, Thomas F., 51
economy of Ireland, 8
Edmundson, John, 87

Ellis, James, 79
Ellis, Mary, 79
emigration, 78
Encumbered Estates Act, 1849, 81
England, 73
    clothing from, 82
entertainment, 24
*Erne,* 51, 53, 78
Erris, 19, 33, 59, 67
Europe, food shortage, 22
Eustace Street, Dublin, 4
Eves:
    Charlotte, 87
    Jane, 87
    Joshua, 87

famine in 1860's, 76
Fayle, Joshua, 51, 52, 53
Fayle, Samuel, 85
Fennell, Mary, 87
Fermanagh, county, 17, 63, 64
    amount of relief, 88
    clothing grants, 44
fever, 78
fish curing, 49, 51
Fisher:
    Abraham, 84
    Thomas, 87
    Thomas W.,76
fisheries, 32, 35, 48, 71, 78
fishermen, 20
fishing, 74
fishing net manufacture, 55
Fitt, Thomas, 85
flannel manufacture, 67
flax, 59,60,62,68
    cultivation, 35
    mill, 60, 62
    scutching mill, 68
Fleet Street, Dublin, No. 43, 15, 71

Martin, William, 74
Mathew, Father, 74
Mayo, 17, 20, 21, 26, 59, 67, 79
    amount of relief, 89
    seed distribution, 46, 47
Meath, county, amount of relief, 88
Meeting for Sufferings, 6
Merchants Quay, Dublin, 44
Mining Company of Ireland, 15
Moate, 67, 69
model farm, 69, 76
Monaghan, county, amount of relief, 88
money grants, amount distributed, 88
Monthly Meeting, 5
Moss, Mary, 87
Mountmellick, 40, 77
    Friends School, 77
Mulvany, William T., 49
Munster, 5, 6, 15, 34, 35, 37
    amount of relief, 89
    Quarterly Meeting, 6


needlework, 67
New Orleans, 22
New York, 21,22,73,78
Newport, county Mayo, 60
Norton, Thomas, junior, 86
Norwich, 17


O'Connell, Maurice, MP, 55
Offaly, (King's County),
    amount of relief, 88
    clothing grants, 43
Ormond Quay, Dublin, 28


pawnbrokers, 40, 48
Perry, Henry, 40, 83, 87
Perry, James, 13, 18, 44, 59, 73, 83

Philadelphia, 21, 22
Pike:
    Amelia, 87
    Ebenezer, 33, 84
    Jonathan, 84
    Wight, 51, 52, 53
Pim:
    Brothers & Co., 71
    James, junior, 83
    John T., 85
    John, junior, 84
    Jonathan, 13, 71, 72, 81, 83
        death of, 81
        elected to parliament, 81
        ill health, 15, 78
        land reform, 81
        photograph, 80
        publications, 26, 81
        visit to Connaught, 18, 21
        writes to American Quakers, 21
    Sophia, 87
    Thomas, 83
    Thomas Thacker, 84
    Thomas, junior, 13, 44, 76, 83
    William Harvey, 83
piracy, 19
poor law, 38
    unions, 35, 36
population, 1
prayers, public, 74
proselytising, lack of, 39
public relief works, 35
publicity, 25
publishing, 25


Quakers:
    American, 11
    effect of famine on, 77
Quarterly Meeting, 5
Queen's College, Galway, 72